A rough guide to the
New Testament

A rough guide
to the New Testament

Simon Jones

Inter-Varsity Press

INTER-VARSITY PRESS
38 De Montfort Street, Leicester LE1 7GP, England

Unless otherwise stated, quotations from the Bible are from the New Revised Standard Version, copyright 1989, Division of Christian Education, National Council of Churches of Christ in the USA.

First published 1994

British Library Cataloguing in Publication Data
A catalogue record for this book is available from the British Library.

ISBN 0-85111-223-4

Set in Linotron Palatino
Photoset in Great Britain by Parker Typesetting Service, Leicester
Printed in Great Britain by Cox & Wyman Ltd, Reading, Berkshire

Inter-Varsity Press is the book-publishing division of the Universities and Colleges Christian Fellowship (formerly the Inter-Varsity Fellowship), a student movement linking Christian Unions in universities and colleges throughout the United Kingdom and the Republic of Ireland, and a member movement of the International Fellowship of Evangelical Students. For information about local and national activities write to UCCF, 38 De Montfort Street, Leicester LE1 7GP.

Contents

List of illustrations

Foreword

This is a book about Jesus – what we know about him and how we know it. It's a book about the letters and stories that Jesus' first followers wrote and collected together to keep a reliable record of what his life, death and resurrection achieved.

The New Testament has been a special book to me for over twenty years, since the day I first encountered its central character, Jesus Christ. I read it avidly and with relish because in it I meet Jesus and through it I get to know him better. I turn to it when I need guidance, need to know right from wrong, want to find out how to pray and how to live.

In my reading over the years I've benefited greatly from teachers and preachers who have explained difficult passages and made its words come alive to me. So I'm dedicating my attempt to introduce people to the world of Jesus and the early church to those men who have done most to take me there: Donald Guthrie, through his writing and friendship, and Dick France, Steve Motyer and Bob Willoughby, who taught me at London Bible College. Not only their words but also their lives spoke to me of the truth of the New Testament. Thanks, guys.

Thanks also to Linda, my wife and keenest critic, for ideas, proof-reading and patience while I've been at the word processor and she's been doing my share of the chores.

Introduction

The New Testament is about Jesus. Christians read it because they believe that in its pages they encounter him, learn what he taught and hear his voice speaking to them.

But Jesus lived 2,000 years ago in a world very different from ours. There were no cars, TVs, telephones, fridges or microwaves. People spoke long-dead languages, wore strange clothes and engaged in even stranger rituals at the meal table.

The action of the New Testament takes place in that world. So, not surprisingly, we find some of what it says puzzling. The New Testament was written to explain Jesus to that world, not ours. The apostles and others who penned the twenty-seven books that make up the New Testament wrote with two purposes in mind.

One was purely domestic. The new movement had problems. The churches, filled with sinners who had been saved through faith in Jesus, were not perfect. Troubles brewed, fights broke out, questions arose about what foods were acceptable and what people should wear to church. The apostles wrote to teach Christians about these and other matters.

The second purpose was that the church wanted to tell the world who Jesus was and what he had achieved through his life, death and resurrection in obscure little Palestine in the first decades of the first century.

Then, after the apostles had written, the church gathered what was felt to be inspired and vital for building future generations of Christians into the collection of books that we call the New Testament.

Your starter for ten

Because of the way in which the New Testament was written, readers today often have questions about it that are less to do with what it means and more to do with why its writers wrote it the way they did. So, why are there four accounts of Jesus' life (the four Gospels), three of which are very similar and one of which is very different? Why did Paul write letters and not short, helpful manuals on Christian living and running churches? How are we to make sense of Revelation?

And then we're intrigued to know who the people were who wrote the New Testament – especially Paul, Luke and John, who wrote so much of it. Where did they live, why did they write?

These are traditionally called 'background questions'. Answering them fills in the background and explains the context in which the books were written so that we can grasp their message more easily.

The point of reading the New Testament is to meet Jesus. Doing a bit of background work helps us to set Jesus and the early Christians firmly and correctly in their context so that we can hear them more accurately and see them more clearly.

How will we get there?

The first two chapters of this book are longer than the rest and sketch in the history of the Israel in which Jesus lived and the century in which the church was born. We will fill in some background on the religious groups in Palestine and the festivals that Jesus would have attended, and we will try to catch the flavour of the everyday life of those times. Then we will move on to show how the church expanded out of Jerusalem and all over the Roman world, and we'll have a stab at saying when things happened and when the New Testament books were written.

From Chapter 3 onwards we will look at the books themselves, starting with the four Gospels, moving through Acts to Paul's letters, glancing at James, Peter, Jude and the writer of Hebrews, and ending up with John's letters and the book of Revelation. Finally there's a brief account of how the New Testament came together.

So you could either read the book through in sequence or jump about finding answers to the questions that you feel are most pressing at the moment. But above all, the aim of this book is to make you want to read the New Testament for yourself. If, having taken our brief tour, you are able to do that with a little more understanding and hence enjoyment and benefit, my labours will have been worthwhile.

CHAPTER 1

■ ■ ■ ■ ■ ■ ■ ■ ■

Jesus' world

A trip through the Palestine where Jesus grew up

████████

Most British people don't know much history. Perhaps we're aware of Churchill and the Second World War. But we know little about the Corn Laws, Chartism, John Wilkes, the Levellers, the Act of Supremacy or the signing of Magna Carta. And yet these events have shaped us and made us the people we are.

Jesus grew up in a community very conscious of its history, of the events that had moulded it and the people who made it what it was. Shakespeare likened history to a tale told by an idiot, full of sound and fury and signifying nothing. Maybe we share his view. To Jesus and his community, history was a tale told by God, full of sin and salvation and working its way to a climax: the coming of God's Kingdom.

Striking a blow for freedom

From about 530 BC onwards the people of Israel drifted back from exile. Nehemiah rebuilt Jerusalem from the

A rough history of Israel

BC

600

Exiles come back from Babylon

500

Ezra and Nehemiah working in Jerusalem

Jerusalem temple rebuilt

400

Alexander the Great conquers the Middle East

Israel swallowed up

~~PTOLEMIES~~
SELUCIDS OK

PTOLEMIES OK

300

Ptolemies rule OK

Selucids replace Ptolemies in Israel

200

Maccabean revolt

Romans take over

100

Herod becomes King of Judea

Jesus born in Bethlehem

0

John the Baptist
Jesus' ministry
Crucifixion

440s. Many Jews never bothered to return. Instead they stayed in the East or made their way west to Turkey, Greece and Italy, living in what came to be known as the Diaspora.

For those who did return life wasn't great, except for one glorious period that people in Jesus' day looked back to as a golden age and an inspiration to all freedom-loving Jews.

The Persian empire of Cyrus and Artaxerxes, which allowed the Jews to return to their land, fell to the expanding Greek empire of Alexander the Great, with Palestine coming under his authority in 332 BC. When Alexander died at the tender age of thirty-two, his empire was torn in two by rival generals: the Ptolemies, based in Egypt, held sway in the South, while the Selucids, based in Syria, held sway in the North. Palestine was the meat in the sandwich between the two power blocks.

To begin with, it was ruled by the Ptolemies, who were live-and-let-live kings. They allowed the Jews, especially around Jerusalem, a great deal of autonomy, provided they paid their taxes. But in 200 BC Palestine was won from the Ptolemies by the Selucids, who were more aggressive rulers. Life for the Jews got harder.

Life became intolerable in the second century under the Selucid ruler, Antiochus IV Epiphanes, whose policy was to force all his subjects to adopt Greek ways. The Jerusalem aristocracy went along with this, but the priestly families and the rural peasant farmers resisted. In 167 BC Antiochus set up a statue to the pagan god Zeus in the temple in Jerusalem and banned the practice of the Jewish religion in Judea.

This sparked off a full-scale revolt in 164, led by Judas Maccabeus, 'the Hammer'. So successful was this uprising that the pagans were driven out of the land and Judea became self-governing. The temple was cleansed and restored – an event still celebrated by Jews today in a festival called Hanukkah.

All roads lead to Rome

At this time the Roman Empire was gaining in strength, and it made sense for the tiny state of Judea to have a powerful friend. So in 139 it signed a treaty with Rome which guaranteed its protection and enabled it to expand. Over the next fifty years the state grew to the size it had been under King David, capturing first Samaria, then the southern Idumean kingdom and then the northern territories of Galilee and the Decapolis, as well as the coastal towns. Its policy was to reverse what the Selucids had done, removing Greek cultural and religious influences and almost forcing people to practise the Jewish religion – which most of them were only too happy to do.

But there were political problems: squabbles and fights between rival groups threatened to reduce the country to anarchy and civil war, and in 63 BC the Romans stepped in and took control of the whole region.

Rome liked, wherever possible, to rule through local kings. So, when it found a powerful and loyal royal family in Idumea, it made them kings of the country. The most famous member of this dynasty is Herod the Great, king when Jesus was born.   *(Luke 1:5)*

Herod sought to win the popularity of his new subjects by rebuilding their temple in Jerusalem and making it one of the wonders of the world. It was still being finished off during Jesus' ministry. Herod did a lot of other public works, but he was an unstable and paranoid man, convinced that every dark corner contained a group plotting his overthrow. He put to death many of his rivals, and even some of his own children. So it is no surprise that, on hearing of Jesus' birth, he had all boys under the age of two in Bethlehem killed for fear of losing his throne to the new rival.   *(Matthew 2:16–18)*

When Herod died his kingdom was divided among

The Herods

Boundary of Herod the Great's kingdom

Judea (Archelaus the ethnarch)

Galilee (Herod Antipas the tetrarch)

Iturea

The rest of the Tetrarchy of Philip

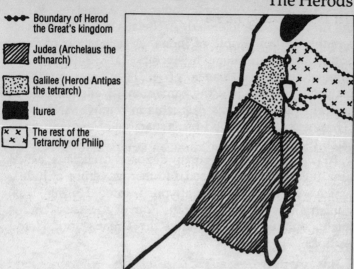

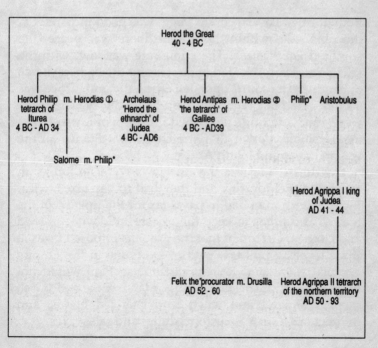

Herod the Great
40 - 4 BC

Herod Philip m. Herodias ①   Archelaus   Herod Antipas m. Herodias ②   Philip*   Aristobulus
tetrarch of   'Herod the   'the tetrarch' of
Iturea   ethnarch' of   Galilee
4 BC - AD 34   Judea   4 BC - AD39
                                4 BC - AD6

Salome m. Philip*

Herod Agrippa I king
of Judea
AD 41 - 44

Felix the procurator m. Drusilla   Herod Agrippa II tetrarch
AD 52 - 60   of the northern territory
                                      AD 50 - 93

17

his sons, Herod Antipas, Philip and Archelaus. While the first two were tolerated, Archelaus was totally unacceptable to the people of Judea. A delegation of Samaritan and Jerusalem aristocrats (an unlikely and somewhat unholy alliance, given the mutual animosity between the Jews and the Samaritans) went to Rome to appeal to the Emperor Augustus to remove Archelaus. (These events lie behind Jesus' parable of the pounds in Luke 19.)

To keep the peace Augustus deposed Archelaus, exiled him to France and imposed a Roman governor of Judea, which was not really what anyone wanted. During Jesus' ministry Judea was ruled by the Roman governor Pontius Pilate, and Galilee by Herod the Great's son, Herod Antipas.

A bit of a curate's egg

Roman rule, like the curate's egg, was good in parts. On the plus side, within the Empire there was peace, the so-called *Pax Romana*. The crime rate was low, with the seas by and large cleared of pirates and the highways free of bandits. The courts operated efficiently and justice was administered in a relatively even-handed way. The roads were good and trade flourished. Many people prospered in the single market that stretched from France all the way to Egypt and North Africa.

The down side was that the Jews were no longer in control of their destiny and they had to pay taxes twice. Every Jewish man had to pay a tax for the upkeep of the temple and tithes to keep the priests and levites in food and clothes. On top of that the Romans imposed taxes at three levels: a poll tax, paid by everyone in the Empire except Italians and Roman citizens (so Paul would not have paid it, but Jesus would); a land tax levied on all owners of land and when land changed hands; and indirect taxes such as customs duties and sales taxes.

18

It is reckoned that the average Jewish man saw about 40% of his income go in taxes. So, not surprisingly, taxation caused huge amounts of aggro, debates about whether it should be paid or not and occasional armed uprisings.

Possibly the biggest bone of contention was the method the Romans used to collect their taxes. Instead of using their own civil servants, they contracted the job out to freelance tax-gatherers who made a lump-sum payment to Rome for the tax due on their patch and then collected that back plus a bit extra from the hapless citizens. Tax-gatherers had all the social standing of prostitutes, lepers and serial killers in first-century Palestine – as we see in the story of Zacchaeus.   *(Luke 19:1–10)*

There was one other benefit of being part of an empire, though this was an accidental spin-off from Alexander's conquest. It was that nearly everyone spoke the same language. Latin was the official language of the Roman Empire, but in the eastern half of the Empire few non-Romans spoke it, though it was the language of the law courts. Greek was the language that everyone spoke in the market-place, so whether you lived in Alexandria in Egypt, Ephesus in Turkey or Nazareth in Galilee, you would have known enough Greek to get by.

This means that Jesus would almost certainly have been able to speak three languages. His everyday teaching and conversation with people in Galilee and Judea would have been in Aramaic. Conversations with people in the Decapolis or with Romans, especially at his trial, would have been in Greek. And when he read in synagogue, he would have spoken Hebrew, the language of the Old Testament.   *(Mark 5:41)*

D'ya wanna be in my gang?

The world of Jesus' day was full of groups, sects, parties and gangs. They were not political parties as we have them today. They were more debating and pressure groups, collections of people coming together to promote a certain view of life, and especially of what it meant to be a Jew, a member of the covenant people of God in first-century Palestine. Some of these groups we come across in the Gospels, others we don't.

The main group we meet in the Gospels are the Pharisees. They get a really bad press from Christians. We tend to see them as fussy hypocrites, but in fact they were the charismatic evangelicals of Jesus' day.

They date from the period of the Maccabean revolt and their name probably means 'separated'. They took the Law of God very seriously and sought to live by it, applying it to every detail of their daily lives. These applications became a sort of supplementary law handed down from teacher to pupil and debated in small groups or fellowships. Their aim was not to invent rules that couldn't be kept but to be as practically holy as possible. *(Luke 6:1–2)*

The Pharisees were not priests. Most of them were ordinary men who wanted their faith to touch the whole of their lives. They were very influenced by apocalyptic ideas (see Chapters 8 and 10), especially by the notion that God would break into history and establish his Kingdom through his anointed king, the Messiah. They believed in the resurrection, in the Holy Spirit and in angels – all quite new ideas within Judaism. They also believed that membership of the people of God was based on grace – God's choice through the covenant – not on works.

They were not very political, though they resented Roman rule, which they felt polluted God's land. When the Kingdom came, they thought, the Romans would be driven out and the land purified. They were very popular and people looked up to them. After the fall of Jerusalem in AD 70 they became the dominant group in the rebuilding of Judaism without a temple.

Alongside the Pharisees were the scribes. As the name suggests, these people were connected with books and learning. They not only wrote but also studied and taught the Law. Their role was to preserve the good traditions of the people of God and guard them against heresy.

Jesus laid into these two groups because of their snobbery and exclusiveness, their belief that only they had God's ear, only they took discipleship seriously. Their sin was pride and a judgmental, condescending attitude to anyone not as perfect or privileged as them.

The final group we come across in the Gospels is the Sadduccees. These were the opposite of the Pharisees. They were part of the ruling elite, Judea's aristocracy. Their power-base was the temple, where most of them were priests. They were very conservative in their views, rejecting such new doctrines as the resurrection. And they considered only the first five books of the Old Testament (the Torah) to be God's Word; the other books were interesting but not authoritative. They weren't very popular among ordinary Jews. Many saw them as too friendly with the Romans, too keen to feather their own nests. No-one mourned their passing with the destruction of the temple in AD 70.   *(Mark 12:18)*

Taking it to extremes

Two other groups are worthy of mention. They fill out the picture, showing the extremes in the debate about what it meant to be the people of God in first-century Judea.

The first group was the Essenes. They were a small, elitist sect who cut themselves off from everyone else by living in a fortified monastery by the Dead Sea. We knew virtually nothing about them until 1948, when some documents (now known as the Dead Sea Scrolls) were discovered in caves at a place called Qumran.

What they revealed was a group who believed that God

Jesus' early life

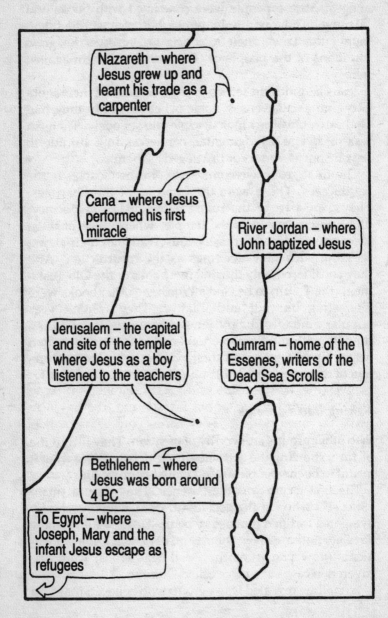

Nazareth – where Jesus grew up and learnt his trade as a carpenter

Cana – where Jesus performed his first miracle

River Jordan – where John baptized Jesus

Jerusalem – the capital and site of the temple where Jesus as a boy listened to the teachers

Qumram – home of the Essenes, writers of the Dead Sea Scrolls

Bethlehem – where Jesus was born around 4 BC

To Egypt – where Joseph, Mary and the infant Jesus escape as refugees would come soon and establish the Kingdom and that only the very purest of Jews would be worthy to enter it. They thought the temple in Jerusalem and the priests who worked in it were hopelessly corrupt, and they dreamed of the day when they would take it over and offer pure sacrifices to God.

As well as living lives of celibacy, they devoted themselves to reading the Scriptures and producing commentaries on them for their own use. They also trained for war, in anticipation of the day when they, the Sons of Light, would fight with God and his angels against the Sons of Darkness, the Romans. In the event, they appear to have been wiped out in AD 70.

The second group are usually known as the Zealots, but this isn't strictly accurate. The Zealots were one of a number of groups at this time who believed that God needed a helping hand in purifying the land and establishing his kingdom. These groups were the militants in first-century Palestine, the PLO of their day.

Through the first half of the century such groups sprang up from time to time: Judas the Galilean led a tax revolt in AD 6; Barabbas was involved in an insurrection at the time of Jesus' crucifixion; Theudas tried to start a revolt in the early 40s in the area around the River Jordan. In the 50s there flourished a group called the Sicarii ('the dagger men') of whom Eleazor and 'the Egyptian' were the most notable. They carried out assassinations and generally got up the Romans' noses.

Jesus' world was a world in ferment. Although life carried on much as normal in most parts of his country, and although it's probably true to say that most people weren't part of any gang, there was an undercurrent of discontent, a desire for something better, a longing that God would come. No wonder Jesus touched a nerve with ordinary people.

Keeping and celebrating the faith

At the heart of Jesus' world as he grew up, worked as a carpenter and travelled as a preacher, were the synagogue and temple. The synagogue was the centre of community life. Every substantial village had one. Not only was it a place of worship on the Sabbath (Saturday), it was also the place where Jewish boys learned to read and recite the law prior to their Bar Mitzvah – the ceremony on their thirteenth birthday in which they became a Son of the Law, an adult member of their community.   *(Luke 4:16)*

Jesus was faithful in his attendance at synagogue and in his participation. Synagogue was run not by priests but by laymen. There were no sacrifices offered; the services consisting rather of the reading of the Law and the Prophets, a sermon, prayers and worship based around the singing of Psalms.

While every town had a synagogue, there was only one temple. It was in Jerusalem, and, as rebuilt by Herod, it was a vast and wonderful building, visible for miles around with its gold dome radiant in the sunlight.

Every day priests served in the temple, offering sacrifices at morning and evening worship. They also made a daily offering for the Emperor, but this practice ceased in AD 66 with the outbreak of the revolt. And from time to time private sacrifices were made on behalf of individuals.   *(Luke 18:10)*

The temple was the focal point of the three big festivals in the Jewish year. The Feast of Passover (including the Feast of Unleavened Bread) happened in March/April and celebrated the Exodus of the people of God from Egypt under Moses. The Feast of Pentecost in May/June celebrated the harvest and the giving of the Law. The Feast of Tabernacles in September/October celebrated the time when the people of God lived in the wilderness in tents. This was the most joyous of the festivals, with all

Major festivals of the Jewish year

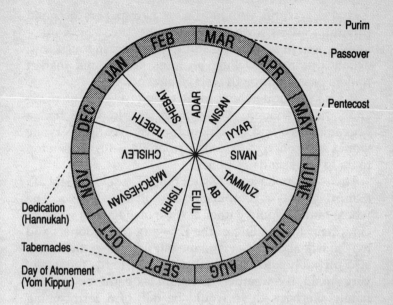

Purim

Passover

Pentecost

Dedication (Hannukah)

Tabernacles

Day of Atonement (Yom Kippur)

(Months shown on wheel: JAN, FEB, MAR, APR, MAY, JUNE, JULY, AUG, SEPT, OCT, NOV, DEC; and TEBETH, SHEBAT, ADAR, NISAN, IYYAR, SIVAN, TAMMUZ, AB, ELUL, TISHRI, MARCHESVAN, CHISLEV)

the people living in tents in the streets or on the flat roofs of their houses. Every day there were parades as the priests brought water into the temple in remembrance of God's provision of water in the desert, and every evening great lights were lit to commemorate God's presence in the pillar of fire.

Every Jew was expected to go to Jerusalem for these festivals. Jesus certainly went on a number of occasions, according to John's Gospel. How many others joined him is anyone's guess. One estimate suggests that the normal population of Jerusalem of 30,000 was swelled to 180,000 at Passover time.   *(John 7:1–10)*

People of the land

Jesus lived in a world where most people earned their living from the land. If they weren't farmers, they were

25

fishermen or the craftsmen who supplied agricultural implements or household goods.

It was a world without TV or newspapers or rapid communications; a world where news spread by word of mouth, where people told stories and kept in touch with events through travelling business people and market traders passing through their village.

It was a world where most people just about made ends meet, though every village would have had a beggar or two and a rich landowner. Nearly everyone would grow enough to feed their family, with a bit on top to trade for essential supplies.

There was not a lot of leisure time. The Jewish Sabbath (Saturday) was a compulsory day off for all Jews. The whole family would gather at the synagogue to worship God, hear the reading of the Law and the Prophets and maybe talk about what it all meant. Of course, there was also probably a lot of talk about crops, herds (generally very small), the weather, taxes and tax-gatherers and the family. Perhaps there would be talk of a forthcoming wedding, or the fact that a son or daughter was now of marriageable age and a suitable partner was being sought.

The rest of the week was hard graft. From dawn till dusk every member of the family would muck in with chores around the house and farm. If the business of the household was manufacturing – such as carpentry – even the youngest would have a role tidying up or making sure that the few animals the family owned were fed and watered.

So it's not surprising that special occasions were an excuse for a party. Weddings lasted a week, with feasting and exchanging of gifts. Banquets – which were rare, and hosted and attended only by the wealthiest in the community – were spectator sports. The guests would recline at low tables in the open courtyard of the house, being waited on by servants who brought not only the food but also warm, scented water for the diners to wash their hands in every so often. A large animal – at least a sheep but at big feasts a cow or ox – would be roasted over an open fire as the guests gathered. Those not invited crowded round the gate to the house, drooling over the sumptuous food and playing 'spot the celebrity' – perhaps the guests would include the synagogue ruler, or a prominent scribe, or the local Roman centurion.   *(John 2:1–11; Luke 7:37–50)*

Other excuses for a celebration would include finding something precious that had been lost, like a sheep or a coin, or paying off the debt incurred to a money-lender because of a poor harvest or broken plough.

It was a world of colourful characters: tax-gatherers, merchants from exotic lands, kings, robbers, victims, helpful travellers, prostitutes, sinners, debtors and insufferably snooty religious people.

It was a world that provided a rich source of material to the gifted preacher looking for illustrations for his teaching about the Kingdom of God. So it's not surprising that this world crops up in vivid colour in all its humour and sadness in Jesus' parables.

For further thought

Look at the parables in Matthew 13:1–10, 24–30, 31–33, 44–50; 18:23–35; 20:1–16; 22:1–14:

(a) What do they tell us about the world in which Jesus lived?

(b) What do they teach us about how to communicate the good news of Jesus to our friends and neighbours?

CHAPTER 2

■■■■■■■■■

Caesar's world

A sprint through the first century

███████

*T*he church was born into a world dominated by Rome in a century which saw the power of the Emperor grow from toughest soldier into god-like ruler. The first Christians benefited from and suffered at the hands of a state that was tolerant of many opinions but would have no truck with divided loyalty: Caesar was Lord, no-one else.

In Chapter 1 we sketched in something of the world in which Jesus lived and worked. In this chapter we are going on a whistle-stop tour of the first century. Like one of those American coach trips that does Europe in six days, there will be no time for dwelling on any year or even decade. But hopefully it will whet your appetite for more, so at the end of the chapter there will be a couple of suggestions for further reading.

Recognizing that some people find history a little dull, we'll take our tour in two ways: first, there's a story. I made it up, but it could have happened. Secondly, we'll sketch in some dates, attempting to show when the

The Roman Empire in New Testament times

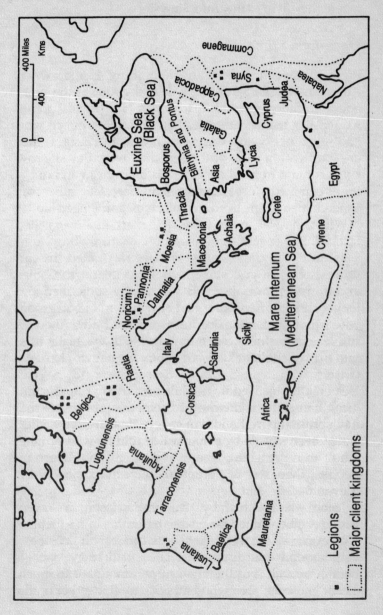

books that make up the New Testament were written and where they fit in to the unfolding story.

Once upon a time . . .

Right at the end of the reign of King Herod, when Augustus was Emperor, the wife of the ruler of the synagogue in Sidon gave birth to a girl. Her proud parents named her Esther, after the Old Testament queen who had saved her people during their exile in Persia. Esther grew up within sight of the sea, and every day she saw ships coming from all over the Mediterranean and camel trains coming to meet them from the East. Her father was a merchant and she lived a comfortable, privileged life.

When she was in her teens, she married a man called Jacob. Like her father, he was a merchant trading cloth, silks and high-class woven fabrics. He traded up and down the coast and sometimes went inland to Galilee and down to Jerusalem. He was a handsome man and Esther thought her father had chosen her a good groom when they first met. But he had a hard edge: he was ruthless in business and many people didn't really trust him – they thought he lived up to his name, Jacob the twister.

Soon after his wedding, while on a trip to Capernaum, Jacob met some men who had joined a new group that had sprung up in the Jordan valley a few months earlier. It had been started by a man called John, a wild prophet who was preaching about judgment and baptizing people in the river as a preparation for the coming of the Messiah.

Jacob was touched by their enthusiasm; like every good Jew, he wanted the Messiah to come in his lifetime. However, he didn't want it to affect his business. Esther's dad was dismissive. There had been prophets before, he said, but they had never amounted to much. There had been men who had got a mob together on the promise that God had chosen them to rid the land of the Romans, but they had been no match for Caesar's well-trained soldiers. 'John's just another flash in the pan,' he told the children.

A couple of years later on another trip, Jacob ran into a crowd making their way up a hill in Galilee to hear another preacher. John's message had given him the odd sleepless night: 'What if what he's saying is true?' he had wondered. 'What does God really think of me?' Normally in the cut and thrust of the day these thoughts never reared their heads, but now he was at a loose end waiting for a camel train of cloth to arrive at the oasis.

Since he was curious, he tagged along. What he saw and heard stunned him. Sick people were healed, blind people were given their sight. A man ran past him shouting, 'Jesus made me clean! Jesus made me clean!' Jacob noticed he was wearing the customary rags of a leper, and yet his skin was perfect.

He never actually got to see Jesus properly because of the crush. But, as he told Esther, this man must be the one John the Baptizer had been talking about. Esther's eyes shone and she spoke excitedly, for she too had heard of this Jesus from a group of men bringing spices down to a ship bound for Athens that very day. She seemed to think that Jesus might be the Messiah. 'Well, I don't know about that,' said Jacob. 'Surely when he comes there'll be more to it than a little healing in the deserts of Galilee.' But he couldn't get the faces of those whom Jesus had healed out of his mind.

Jacob wanted to find out more, but business kept him at home for months. Next time he went to Galilee, Jesus was gone. He had travelled south to Jerusalem with his message of God's rule coming soon, and there he had been opposed by the authorities, betrayed by a friend and crucified. 'It all happened months ago,' said one customer. 'We had hopes, but . . .' He shrugged. 'Nothing's going to change, is it?' Maybe Esther's dad had been right after all. But to Jacob's surprise Jesus' fate disturbed and upset him more than he expected. It seemed an unjust end to one who had only done good.

Days of hope

When Jacob returned home, several weeks later, Esther wasn't there. Her mother was preparing food in the courtyard and her father was sitting in the shade of a vine. 'She's in the market square,' he said. 'There's quite a commotion. Something about Jesus, another prophet, this time from Nazareth.'

Jacob was about to say what had happened to Jesus when Esther burst in. 'Oh Jacob!' she cried. 'There's a man talking about Jesus in the market square . . .'

'But Jesus is dead and buried,' Jacob cut in.

'No, he's not. He was crucified, but God raised him from death and then gave his Spirit to his followers. Something wonderful is happening, Jacob, I can feel it.'

Jacob went to the market-place, where Nicolaus from Jerusalem was preaching to a crowd of a hundred or so. Jacob was all set to shout out that Jesus was dead and gone, when he heard about what had happened after the crucifixion – how his followers had seen him alive on many occasions, spoken to him, eaten with him, and how, after Jesus had returned to heaven, the Holy Spirit had come and filled his followers with new life, energy, joy and hope, and how a new movement had started in his name.

Jacob was struck dumb by all this. But then, rising from his stomach he felt such a thrill that he thought he was going to burst. He wanted to shout it from the roof-tops: 'Jesus *is* alive!' He turned to Esther, tears streaming down his face, and embraced her. He kept saying over and over, 'It's true, it's true. I feel it. I feel him, his life and energy in me!' Suddenly his business, which had been everything he had lived for, seemed less important than letting people – his friends, neighbours, family – know the wonderful things that God had done through Jesus.

Going to the ends of the earth

He had a trip to Antioch planned that would take him away from home for months. Esther wanted to come too, and nothing her bewildered father or Jacob said would dissuade her. So they set off with Nicolaus and a few of his group who wanted to take the news of Jesus up the coast.

It was an exciting trip. Hundreds of people along the way wanted to know about Jesus, and quite a few of them were interested in Jacob's cloth too – without him having to use any of his old tricks to get people to buy! But by the time they reached Antioch Jacob was preaching virtually full-time, and Esther was telling everyone she met about Jesus. Amazingly, she didn't seem to care who heard the story – Jews or Gentiles, all were welcome. Jacob wasn't so sure, but he couldn't deny that when Gentiles wanted to follow Jesus, God gave them his Spirit just as he had done with the Jewish believers.

They found a hall for meetings, and one of the team got a message back to Jerusalem calling for help in teaching all the new believers. Jacob and Esther found lodging with a Gentile family who had become followers. And because their house was so big they were able to hold meetings there for those who wanted to find out more and worship God the Jesus way.

It was there that Esther met Barnabas, who had come from Jerusalem, and Paul, who had been drafted in by Barnabas to help teach and care for all the new converts. Paul was small but fiery, committed and single-minded – like Jacob had been about his business, but honest and kind. Jacob warmed to him and spent a great deal of time

A rough New Testament history

Augustus
(Roman Emperor 43BC – AD14)

Death of Herod the Great
(Kingdom divided into three)

BC

10

0

Jesus born in Bethlehem

10

Reign of Tiberius

20

Baptism of Jesus

30

Conversion of Paul

Jesus' death and resurrection

Reign of Caligula

Reign of Claudius

40

Paul's first missionary journey

The Jerusalem Council

Paul's second missionary journey

50

Reign of Nero

Paul's third missionary journey

Paul in prison in Caesarea

60

Paul at Rome

Reign of Vespasian

70

Persecution of church under
Domitian

80

90

100

talking to him about their new faith. Paul spoke with passion about how God had sent Jesus as the Messiah or Christ to deal with sins and create one new people out of Jews and Gentiles. In the course of one sermon he told them how he had been in the market the other day and had met a group who described him as 'a Christian'. 'I like that,' he said. 'I like the fact that people know me as someone who follows Christ.'

The church in Antioch grew, and Jacob and Esther felt they ought to go to other places where the news had not yet been told. So they set off with Paul and Barnabas and headed for Turkey. For nearly twenty years Jacob and Esther travelled, supported by Jacob's business, telling people about Jesus and starting churches in cities around the Turkish coast.

Esther never ceased to be amazed at the change in Jacob. Previously he had been mean and selfish, but now he was a generous man. Often he would feed beggars and sometimes he would give the proceeds of a sale to a family in the church which had hit hard times.

'Who'd have thought it, eh, Jacob?' she said. 'You used to think that the poor only had themselves to blame and that anyone who gave his money away was robbing his family.'

'Yes, I know,' he replied wistfully. 'But then I didn't know how poor I was or how in debt to God. Recently Paul and I had an argument about who had been the worse sinner before we met Jesus. It ended in a draw, because we agreed that it didn't matter how sinful we had been – what mattered was how completely forgiven we are now. And because that's true I can't turn my back on people in need now.'

Esther hugged him and kissed his cheek: 'You're so much nicer now as well!' They both laughed.

They were getting on in years and the time had come for them to settle somewhere. They chose Ephesus because they had lots of friends there, there was a thriving church and there were plenty of contacts for Jacob's trade.

Far away in Rome awful things were happening. The Emperor Nero, who people said was unstable and cruel, had started persecuting the Christians. They had never been popular. Around the Empire at various times there had been opposition; some people had even died. But this was different. Horrific tales reached Jacob and Esther of Christians being burned, torn apart by wild animals and slaughtered in the gladiatorial games.

Worse was to come. Their friend Timothy arrived one stormy night with news that Paul had been beheaded, along with Peter, one of Jesus' first followers. Esther and Jacob were heartbroken. The church was in a state of shock. They had all looked to Paul for leadership. Now he was gone. Jacob was also worried. He'd had a few beatings, and that hadn't perturbed him because he'd always been sure that the state would ensure that the Christians got a fair hearing. Now he wasn't so sure. He feared for Esther too, and for the first time felt relief that they'd been unable to have children. Jesus' words about taking up one's cross suddenly became frighteningly real.

Taking their lead from Nero, local officials began making life harder for the church, and neighbours who had just about tolerated the Christians next door now began to accuse them of being disloyal to the Empire and doing unspeakable things in secret. Esther was beaten up by a group of men led by an off-duty soldier – but, mercifully, not badly.

The news from Israel was pretty bad too. Discontent at Roman rule had boiled over into terrorism and now into a full-scale rebellion. Rome was merciless in its response: the army destroyed Jerusalem, including the temple, and drove the rebels to Herod's old fort at Massada by the Dead Sea. They held out for a while, but when it became clear that the situation was hopeless, that God wasn't going to rescue them, they killed themselves rather than fall into the Romans' hands.

Into the last days

These were dark days of turmoil and confusion. The Roman authorities were still suspicious of the Christians, but they were also wary of the Jews. The Jews never had been able to tolerate Christians, and viewed them as heretics. Now they resented the fact that when they had risen against Rome, the church, led by James, had made itself scarce by leaving Jerusalem and going to Pella up in the Decapolis.

Esther believed that these events had been foreseen by Jesus, that God was acting against Jerusalem because of its unbelief. The church at Ephesus was now the base for John, one of the original twelve apostles, who was teaching and writing in the city. Esther admired him greatly, and Jacob acted as his secretary occasionally.

But life was far from easy for the Christians. Domitian, the new Emperor, began to insist that all his subjects treat him as a god. The oath of loyalty – 'Caesar is Lord' – was not one a Christian could swear with a clear conscience. So ugly stories which had been circulating about Christian practices – drinking blood, eating babies, rejecting the gods of Rome, denying Caesar's right to rule – began to be believed by more and more people.

'I'm not swearing that kind of oath to any man,' declared Jacob. 'Things are getting pretty serious when mere mortals claim to be divine. We must pray for boldness. Life's bound to get harder.'

'We're in God's hands, my love,' said Esther. 'Soon we'll be called home to meet Jesus face to face. What could be better?'

'You're right, as ever. God could not have given me a wiser, more loving companion and partner. And we've had a good life, haven't we?'

Frail and increasingly unable to get about, Esther and Jacob spent a great deal of time at home. People visited. Many came to hear the good news from them and every day the elderly couple would pray with Jews and Gentiles seeking to know God for themselves.

One night some soldiers and an official from the town clerk's office came to the house. Esther flashed a concerned glance to Jacob as they swaggered in. They taunted the old couple and mocked their faith. Jacob stood up and began to tell them about the love of Jesus, about how he had died for their sins. But one of them, a burly, thick-set man with leather straps around his wrists, slapped him across the face. Jacob was sent crashing to the floor. Esther screamed. But Jacob, propping himself up on an elbow and wiping the blood from his mouth on his hand, said firmly: 'Esther! Be strong! We're in God's hands.' The burly man landed a kick squarely on his cheek and Jacob's head whipped back. He lay groaning on the floor. The gang turned its attention to Esther, hitting the old woman with sticks until she crumpled to the floor. They set fire to the house and left. Esther and Jacob died in the flames. The church mourned the loss of a precious couple who had followed the Way from the very beginning.

Now, back to reality

Though Esther and Jacob never existed, thousands like them did – people whose lives were radically changed by the life of an obscure preacher who died in his thirties in the back of beyond, in a country which no-one paid much attention to most of the time.

Jesus was born at the tail-end of the reign of Herod, when Augustus was Emperor, probably around 4 BC. His birth was no big deal as far as the Romans were concerned, though Herod was sent into a blind panic by it. Jesus grew up in a world where Roman power was taken

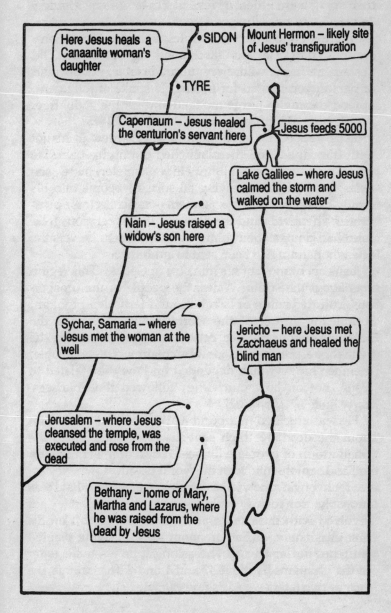

for granted, but in a country where people longed to be free to govern themselves. *(Luke 2:1–2; Matthew 2:1–11)*

John the Baptist, a cousin of Jesus, began his ministry around AD 28. He was like something out of the Old Testament: hairy, wild, fiery, unpredictable, not the kind of person you invited for lunch. He spoke of judgment, of God coming to purge the land and set the godly free. People buzzed with excitement. *(Luke 3:1–15)*

Jesus popped up some months later, threw in his lot with the Baptist and then launched out on his own. He was very different from John. He was quieter, more sociable, spoke of God drawing all sorts of people into his family, people who were sinners – tax-collectors, prostitutes, shepherds and the like – as well as religious folk. John had doubts about him but, it appeared, he was the one whom John had been sent to announce.

Jesus spent most of his ministry in Galilee. This region was about the size of Wales; the people in the prosperous, cultured south of Israel, around Jerusalem, thought it was the armpit of the world. Jesus challenged the religious elite of his day, centred on the temple and the synagogue. He said God was creating a new people, membership of which depended on how they related to Jesus, not on how much they followed the Pharisees' party line. *(Mark 2:22)*

He was crucified in around AD 30, but God raised him from the dead. He then sent his Holy Spirit on to the small group of people who believed in him, set them on fire and sent them to turn the world upside down.

Stephen was martyred a couple of years later. Paul was probably converted within weeks of that. He got involved with the church at Antioch and set off on his first missionary journey in about AD 43. Having planted churches in Galatia and Thessalonica, he wrote his letter to the Galatians in about 47 and 1 and 2 Thessalonians a year or two later. *(Acts 7:54–60; 9:1–19)*

While Paul was pushing into Gentile territory, Peter and James were working in Judea, and other apostles and preachers were planting churches in Samaria and Galilee. James wrote his letter to new Christians and their communities in the late 40s.

Tensions were growing between Jewish Christians and Gentile converts, so a meeting was called in 48 or 49. The so-called Jerusalem council, reported in Acts 15, set the pattern for amicable relations between Jewish and Gentile churches and set the stage for a massive expansion of the church both geographically and numerically in the 50s.

Through that decade Paul and others travelled widely, preaching the gospel and planting churches in cities all over the Empire. Some of Paul's letters to churches were written in this decade – notably to Corinth and Rome – as he tried to keep the new converts on the straight and narrow, giving them teaching and sorting out problems.

Christians didn't face much persecution at this time. Some Jews opposed Paul and made life hard for him, but the Empire was a pretty tolerant place, since there were lots of religions around. So while Christians were victims of anti-Semitism – because people saw the church as a sect within Judaism – by and large they were free to preach and teach and hold meetings.

Things changed towards the end of the decade and into the 60s. The Emperor Nero, an unstable, paranoid, cruel man, used the Christians as scapegoats after the disastrous burning of Rome, for which he was being blamed. In a sudden explosion of ferocity against the church in the mid-60s, Paul and Peter were executed, and thousands of Christians died for no other reason than the faith they held.

While awaiting execution, Paul wrote letters to Timothy and probably to the churches at Ephesus and Colosse. Peter too and his close colleague Jude were sending letters to the churches in Turkey in which they had worked in the early 60s.

In Israel the 60s were also a disastrous decade. Growing resentment against Roman rule exploded in a rebellion in AD 66. The Roman response was savage: Jerusalem was destroyed in AD 70 and the Jews were scattered.

Into the wide blue yonder

From the 70s into the 80s the church enjoyed a respite from official persecution and continued to grow. We know very little about how it was developing. But from the letters of John, which tell us about the church around Ephesus at this time, we know that there were false teaching and leadership problems in the church, though external pressures were slight. We also know that many remained loyal to the teaching of Jesus which had been handed down by the apostles and which was now being preached by a new generation of people whose sins had been forgiven and whose lives had been turned upside down through the cross.

The peaceful years ended with the beginning of the reign of the Emperor Domitian in AD 81. He insisted on people swearing loyalty to him as a god. Failure to do so landed people in hot water.

It seems likely that the apostle John fell foul of Domitian in the mid-80s and was exiled to Patmos. In the book of Revelation, which was written while he was there, we have a searing critique of the Roman state: it is described as a beast that is out of control, persecuting the church and under the judgment of God. Revelation is also a clarion-call to the church to remain faithful to Jesus and to bear witness to his saving grace, even at the risk of losing liberty or life itself, for the gospel says that Jesus and not Caesar is Lord of all.

The century closed with the church under increasing pressure. Under the Emperor Trajan (who ruled from 98 to 117), simply being a Christian seems to have been a capital offence.

But many thousands had been touched and changed by the life and message of Jesus Christ. The good news of Jesus was like yeast. It was now at work in the dough of the Empire. Eventually, it was to take over the world that had tried so fiercely to snuff it out. For, although the Christians remained a persecuted minority for the next two centuries, the church grew and the message gained respect.

Finally, Constantine, almost certainly through the influence of his mother, became a Christian in the early fourth century. When he became Emperor in 312, having defeated all opposition to his claim, he ascribed his victory to the God Jesus Christ, and so Christianity became an official religion of the Empire.

The new acceptance enabled the church to sort itself out and make sure that it was remaining true to the original gospel. Various councils meeting over the next 150 years or so resolved doctrinal problems and gathered the writings that everyone agreed were specially inspired by God into a collection known as the New Testament.

Since those years, as countless generations have come and gone, the gospel of Jesus Christ has remained unchanged in both its content and in its power to transform people's lives. And now in our generation, this message is still turning people's lives upside down and inside out. Today there are many people who would agree with what Paul told the Christians in Rome: 'I am not ashamed of the gospel; it is the power of God to everyone who has faith.'   *(Romans 1:16)*

And finally

The dates in our whistle-stop tour are approximate – being certain about any but a few key dates is impossible. But if your appetite has been whetted for a longer, more detailed tour, then why not look at Paul Barnett's *Bethlehem to Patmos: The New Testament Story* (Hodder &

When the New Testament books were written

AD

| 40 | 50 | 60 | 70 | 80 | 90 |

Galatians

1 & 2 Thessalonians

James

1 Corinthians

2 Corinthians

Romans

Ephesians

Colossians

Philemon

1 Peter

Philippians

2 Peter

Jude

1 Timothy

Titus

2 Timothy

Hebrews

1, 2, 3 John

— Acts —

Revelation

— Synoptic Gospels —

— John's Gospel —

Stoughton, 1989) or F. F. Bruce's *New Testament History* (Marshall Pickering, 3rd edition, 1982)?

For further thought

Think about the world you live in, the church you attend and the world of Esther and Jacob which you have just read about.
(a) What are the similarities?
(b) What are the differences?
(c) Is being a Christian the same now as it was then?

CHAPTER 3

■■■■■■■■■

Put that in triplicate

Matthew, Mark and Luke

'*S*o tell me who this Jesus was, then.' The man holding the sausage roll in one hand and the mug of tea in the other was serious. He knew nothing about Jesus. And why should he? After all, Jesus lived in Israel in the first century, he lives in Camberwell in the twentieth, and no-one has ever introduced them.

As the church grew and spread around the Roman Empire, Christians met more and more people who said, 'So tell me who this Jesus was, then.' And so, they passed on the stories about Jesus which they had been told, or they recalled the events which they themselves had witnessed.

Someone might have recalled the miraculous catch of fish as an example that Jesus had authority over nature. Someone else might have remembered the way Jesus touched lepers and healed them, showing his love and power. Another might have described the fiery way Jesus had spoken about the religious leaders of his day.
(*Luke 5:4–8, 12–13, 11:37–53*)

Soon after the church had exploded on to an unsuspecting world, some people began to collect these stories about Jesus – stories that showed people what he was like and why we should follow him. No doubt every week, as the Christians gathered for worship, various stories about Jesus would be told. It is almost certain that every week the story of Jesus' death and resurrection would be told and remembered as the Christians shared bread and wine together.

Eventually – probably sometime in the 50s or 60s – all these stories were gathered together and edited into collections and books. Our New Testaments open with four of these collections or Gospels. Three of them – Matthew, Mark and Luke – are very similar. They are known as the Synoptic Gospels, and they are the subject of this chapter.

At the beginning of his Gospel, Luke explains his reason for writing:

> *Since many have undertaken to set down an orderly account of the events that have been fulfilled among us, just as they were handed on to us by those who from the beginning were eye-witnesses and servants of the word, I too decided, after investigating everything carefully from the very first, to write an orderly account for you, most excellent Theophilus, so that you may know the truth concerning the things about which you have been instructed.* (Luke 1:1–4)

'The facts, Lewis, give me the facts'

Lots of people had put pen to parchment by the time Luke started. But Luke, who had not known Jesus in the flesh, wanted to check it out for himself. He also wanted to provide an accurate picture of Jesus for Theophilus, possibly a recent wealthy convert who was footing the bill for Luke's enterprise. He was a bit like Lewis filling

Inspector Morse in at the beginning of a case: woe betide him if he didn't get his facts straight!

So Luke set about 'investigating everything carefully'. It is possible that he was able to do this during the two-year period in the late 50s in which Paul, with whom Luke frequently travelled and for whom he may have acted as a secretary, was in prison in Caesarea.

During that time Luke could well have travelled south into Galilee, where Jesus had lived most of his life. There Luke would have talked to people about Jesus. Almost certainly he talked to Jesus' family, maybe even to Mary, about the events surrounding Jesus' birth – for only Luke records them.

It is also quite likely that he had a copy of Mark's Gospel, or at least a version of something very like Mark's Gospel which provided the order in which the key events of Jesus' life and ministry happened.

But Luke's Gospel is more than just a list of events, an account of what happened in Jesus' life. It was written with a very definite purpose: to explain who Jesus was, the significance of his coming and especially the meaning of his death and resurrection.

The Gospels are not biographies of Jesus, like the ones we might read about a rock or movie star, politician or missionary pioneer. Modern biographies give exhaustive (and often exhausting!) details of their subject's home life and schooling, pastimes and hobbies, love-life and contribution to history.

No-one wrote that sort of biography in the ancient world. Ancient writers were not much interested in personal details about their subjects – their psychology, their family relationships, their favourite foods. They were much more interested in their exploits. So the biographies of the Roman Emperors were full of accounts of battles and treaties and stories of how their lives were models of virtuous behaviour.

Well, the Gospels are a bit like that. They concentrate

on telling us what Jesus did and said. They show us clearly that he lived a good and God-honouring life. But they go further than that.

'Walk this way, please . . .'

The Gospels' prime purpose is to show us why we should put our faith in Jesus as the Son of God and the Saviour of the world. The authors are not writing light entertainment, stirring tales or even a moving account of a great religious leader. They are calling readers to put their faith in Jesus, to follow him, to live in the way he lived and to become part of the family he founded – that is, the church.

So Mark begins his account like this: 'The beginning of the good news [or gospel] of Jesus Christ, the Son of God'. Before the word 'gospel' meant a type of book, it meant the proclamation of what God had done and was doing through Jesus. As Paul says, 'The gospel . . . is the power of God for salvation to everyone who has faith.'   *(Mark 1:1; Romans 1:16)*

But this does not mean that the Gospels are fairy stories. That's why Luke stresses to Theophilus that he has carefully investigated what happened, he has talked to eyewitnesses, he has weighed one story with another and has distilled the fruit of all his enquiries into an account that is 'the truth'. And, of course, we now believe that the Holy Spirit was helping him with his enquiries.

Finding our way through the story

So Luke, Matthew and Mark offer us an outline of Jesus' life and ministry that stresses why we should believe that he is the Son of God and the Saviour of the world. John's Gospel has the same purpose but is written in a different style (more on this in the next chapter).

A rough outline of the life of Jesus

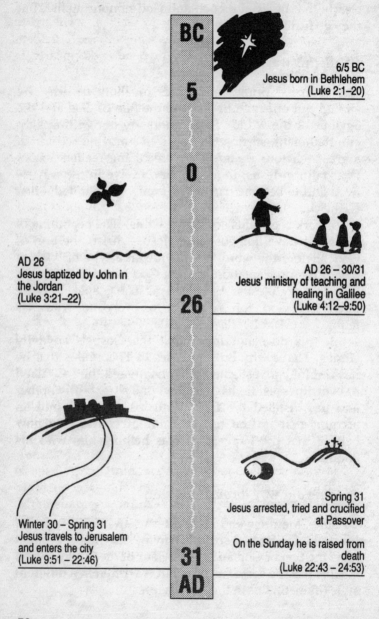

BC

5

0

26

31

AD

6/5 BC
Jesus born in Bethlehem
(Luke 2:1–20)

AD 26
Jesus baptized by John in
the Jordan
(Luke 3:21–22)

AD 26 – 30/31
Jesus' ministry of teaching and
healing in Galilee
(Luke 4:12–9:50)

Winter 30 – Spring 31
Jesus travels to Jerusalem
and enters the city
(Luke 9:51 – 22:46)

Spring 31
Jesus arrested, tried and crucified
at Passover

On the Sunday he is raised from
death
(Luke 22:43 – 24:53)

The basic outline of the gospel story is this: Jesus was baptized by John in the Jordan, carried on a ministry of teaching, healing and exorcism in Galilee, went up to Jerusalem for the Passover, was arrested and crucified. On the third day he rose from the dead and appeared to his disciples.

Within this basic outline, the Synoptic writers tell stories about Jesus' teaching and exploits that confirm their claim that he was the Son of God. All of them tell of the time when Jesus fed 5,000 people with a little boy's packed lunch, of the time when he calmed a fierce storm that blew up on the Sea of Galilee, and of the time when he rode into Jerusalem on a donkey, in conscious fulfilment of Old Testament prophecy about a coming king.

All the Gospels picture Jesus telling great stories with punchlines that made the listeners either hoot with laughter or else wince with recognition that the sinner or the hypocrite or the foolish girl was actually them. We call these stories parables, and even 2,000 years later they have not lost their power to make us think, repent and return to God with renewed faith and gratitude.

To this basic outline Matthew and Luke add details and stories not found in Mark. For instance, both give an account of Jesus' birth, stressing, through different aspects of the event, that he was born in fulfilment of the promises of God contained in the Old Testament. All the Gospel writers are keen to show that there is a strong link between the history of Israel and the ministry of Jesus.   (Matthew 1–2; Luke 1–2)

Matthew seems to have had a great interest in Jesus as a teacher and gathers large quantities of his teaching into various sections of his Gospel. The most famous is the Sermon on the Mount which is found in chapters 5 – 7. But there's also a collection of parables in chapter 13, a section of teaching on relationships between disciples in chapter 18 and a large chunk of material on the future in chapters 23 and 24.

Luke, on the other hand, had a keen sense of what makes a gripping story. He composed his Gospel in such a way as to heighten the drama, especially the sense of growing conflict between Jesus, the Galilean rabbi and the Jewish authorities, whose centre of power was in Jerusalem. The middle section of his Gospel, 9:51 to 19:28, which contains many stories not found in any other gospel, describes Jesus' journey from the northern territory of Galilee, where he had a reputation and was even something of a hero, south to Jerusalem, the capital, the place where his opponents called the shots. As this journey brings him closer and closer to Jerusalem the tension is electrifying.

Getting to the heart of the story

All the Gospels devote a large amount of space to the last week of Jesus' life. The last five and a half chapters of Luke, the last six chapters of Mark and the last eight chapters of Matthew are devoted to Jesus' last week and its aftermath. So great is the stress on these final seven days that some people have suggested that the Gospels are really passion narratives (*i.e.* stories of Jesus' death and resurrection) with brief scene-setting introductions.

This is an exaggeration, of course. But each Gospel focuses on Jesus' final week with an intensity not turned on any other event in his life. The reason for this is simple: the death and resurrection of Jesus lie at the very heart of the good news that Christians want to proclaim to the world.

So the Gospel writers spell out in detail what happened: the last meal, the betrayal of Jesus by one of the Twelve, his anguished prayer in the garden of Gethsemane, his arrest, Peter's denial, his trial before the Jewish authorities (the high priest and council of elders), his trial before Pilate, and his crucifixion. Each Gospel tackles it slightly differently, and Luke adds that Jesus

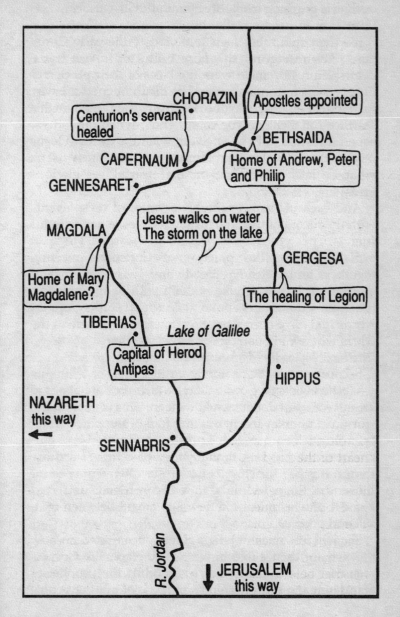

was also seen by Herod, king of Galilee. But the basic outline is the same in all three Synoptic Gospels.
(Luke 23:6–12)

It's clear that these facts mattered to the early Christians. The reason for this is not difficult to see: Jesus' death and resurrection were the basis of their proclamation of salvation in his name. His death opened the way for God to forgive anyone who put their trust in his sacrifice for them on the cross. Thus, while the letters, especially those of Paul, spell out what the death of Jesus means, the Gospel writers carefully and accurately tell us what actually took place on that fearful yet glorious Friday.

And each of them opens his account of these events with the record of the final meal which Jesus had with his friends. They probably did this for two reasons. Firstly, it explains where the practice of Christians meeting together and sharing bread and wine originated. Matthew, Mark and Luke – along with Paul – preserve the words that Jesus spoke at the first Lord's Supper, words that have been used ever since, everywhere in the world where Christians break bread together.
(Matthew 26:26–30; Mark 14:12–26; Luke 22:7–38)

Secondly, it is the Synoptic writers' way of telling us what the events of Good Friday, which they are about to set out for us in detail, actually mean. This is not just the story of a popular teacher falling foul of the powers that be, being falsely accused, unjustly condemned and outrageously executed – though it is, of course, all those things. It is also the story of how Jesus offered himself for the sins of the world, how in his broken body and shed blood God was making a new agreement between himself and people.

So, whereas ancient biographies concentrated on how the lives of their subjects were exemplary, the Gospels focus on how the death of Jesus fulfils the prophecies about him and achieves God's purpose of putting people right with himself and offering them new life.

But of course, the Gospels don't end with Jesus in the grave. A dead Messiah, for all his grand words about giving himself for others, would be no Messiah at all.

Each of the Gospels reaches its climax with an empty tomb and a risen Jesus showing himself to his followers on numerous occasions and in various places. Jesus is alive, they declare. What man did on Good Friday, God reversed on Easter Day. While Mark almost certainly left it there (his Gospel originally ending at 16:8), Matthew and Luke go on to tell us that the risen Jesus commanded his followers to go and tell the world the news of his death and resurrection, the news of forgiveness and new life.   *(Matthew 28; Mark 16:1–8; Luke 24)*

Are you sitting comfortably?

The Gospels seem to have been written primarily to teach newly converted Christians about the founder of their faith. The material is presented in bite-sized chunks, each containing an insight into Jesus' life and character or a slice of his teaching on how to live as his disciple in the world.

It seems that from a very early stage – almost certainly before AD 100 – the Synoptic Gospels were being used in the weekly worship of the church. They offered every Christian believer access to the earthly life of Jesus. Then, as now, they inspired, challenged and nourished the faith of ordinary men and women who, in their daily lives, were seeking to live as he lived.

So the man with the sausage roll who says, 'Tell me who this Jesus was, then' needs to hear the stories Matthew, Mark and Luke told in the lively, honest way they told them.

For further thought

Although Matthew, Mark and Luke wrote basically the same story, they wrote for slightly different reasons. What is distinctive about each writer's portrait of Jesus? (You might find it useful to use a study Bible or commentary to help you with this.)

Read Matthew 16:13 – 17:13, Mark 8:27 – 9:13 and Luke 9:18–36.

(a) What are the differences between the ways in which the writers tell these stories?

(b) What do we learn from the stories?

CHAPTER 4

■■■■■■■■■

Now make it a quartet

John's Gospel

■■■■■■■

A tune played on a piano using only the right hand begins to pall after a while. You think to yourself, 'That's pretty, but couldn't it be more interesting?' Then the pianist begins using her left hand, adding a bass line. And instead of merely playing single notes with the right hand, she plays chords. All of a sudden you're listening to a symphony – well, almost!

In some ways the Synoptic Gospels, which we looked at in the last chapter, are like a tune tapped out with a single finger of the right hand. They give us a line-sketch of Jesus. It is very interesting, but much of the depths in Jesus' character and personality are only hinted at and not really filled out in detail. We find ourselves asking for more.

Then we get to John. John is to the Synoptics what the left hand and chords are to the simple one-finger piano tune. John fills out the Synoptic portrait of Jesus by adding depth and breadth to the picture. John's Gospel was probably the last to be written, though the stories that are unique to it probably circulated from the earliest days of the church. It is probably also the only Gospel to have been written by one of the twelve disciples of Jesus. It has all the hallmarks of being the account of an eye-witness. It is full of little details that suggest the author saw and heard, felt and took part in the stories he is telling.

'Tell us another, Grandpa'

Tradition has it that John wrote his Gospel in Ephesus when he was an old man. It was as if all the other Gospels had come out and had topped the Christian best-seller lists, and John's friends were saying to him, 'Come on, you tell 'em what you know.' Eventually, after much persuading, he took up his pen or dictated his memories and stories to a secretary.

John probably knew of the Synoptic Gospels. He knew what was in them. He knew who they were written for. He did not want to produce yet another book that said the same things to a similar audience.

Mark and Luke wrote in answer to questions from mainly Gentile converts about the founder of Christianity; they wanted to know what Jesus was like. John, on the other hand, like Matthew, appears to have written with mainly Jewish Christians in mind.

The situation was probably something like this. In the final quarter of the first century, after the Romans had destroyed Jerusalem in AD 70, the scattered Jews struggled to keep their faith and traditions alive. At the same time, the Christian church was staking its claim to be a religion separate from both the Judaism it had sprung from and the paganism that it encountered in every city of the Roman Empire.

Jewish Christians – people who had been born Jews but who had come to believe that Jesus was the Messiah promised by the Old Testament – felt squeezed. On the one hand, Gentile Christians were not adopting many of the practices that they thought were important: circumcision, the Old Testament dietary laws, and keeping the Sabbath. On the other hand, the leaders of Judaism were stressing that you could not be loyal to your Jewish roots and accept the claims made by Christians about Jesus of Nazareth.

Many of these Jewish Christians were in danger of losing their faith. Until John wrote his Gospel. What they needed to hear was not the basic story of who Jesus was, what he did, how he died and that he rose again. They knew all that from other sources. What they needed was a fresh angle on Jesus' story that would answer their specific needs.

'It's the way you tell 'em'

Two visitors to Britain, who know nothing of the country's life, politics or culture, decide to find out what's going on by buying a national daily newspaper. One buys the *Daily Mirror*, the other *The Independent*. Were they to compare notes, they would probably wonder if they had been reading about the same country.

Of course, there is overlap between the content of the *Mirror* and *The Independent*. Where they cover the same story, they usually agree on the basic outline of the facts. That they are very different papers – in tone, content and layout – is due to the fact that they are written for very different audiences. The questions an *Independent* reader is asking are very different from those posed by a reader of the *Mirror*.

Perhaps this helps us to get the differences between John and the Synoptics in proportion. Where all four Gospels write about the same event, they agree totally on the basic outline. What they differ on is the level of information provided: John goes into far more detail. This can be seen by comparing the accounts in all four

Gospels of, for example, the feeding of the 5,000 and the trial of Jesus.   *(John 6:1–15; Matthew 14:13–21)*

John leaves out many things that Matthew, Mark and Luke tell us about. He is silent about the birth and baptism of Jesus, the calling of the Twelve, the exorcisms, the parables, the Transfiguration and the institution of the Lord's Supper. But, as we have already noted, he probably didn't feel compelled to include any of these because three other books in circulation already told believers about them.

And as he himself says, there are 'many other things that Jesus did; if every one of them were written down, I suppose that the world itself could not contain the books that would be written'. In other words, he has to be selective and there's no point going over old ground. Especially when he has so many wonderful stories that the others left out of their accounts: the turning of water into wine, the raising of Lazarus, the healing of the man at the pool of Beth-zatha, Jesus' early ministry in Judea and his frequent visits to Jerusalem.   *(John 20:30; 21:25)*

Speaking from experience

There have been a number of histories written about the government of Britain under Harold Wilson. Two of them illustrate the difference between John and the Synoptic Gospels. Recently Ben Pimlot has produced a huge, detailed and magisterial account of the Wilson years. No stone is left unturned, no document unexamined, no participant in or observer of those days uninterviewed. But Pimlot was not a member of that government. In that respect he is like Luke. Tony Benn, on the other hand, has produced a series of volumes of his diaries, written while he was a member of Wilson's cabinet, a participant in events and decisions. In that respect he is like John.

John was an eyewitness. The author of the Gospel was the son of Zebedee, the brother of James, Jesus' best friend on earth, the only one of the inner circle to put pen to paper. This, no doubt, made him much more confident about his material. Matthew, Mark and Luke would not include anything in their Gospels that they weren't absolutely sure of, that they couldn't actually check out – hence the short speeches of Jesus, the easily remembered one-sentence sayings, the briefly told incidents.

John, on the other hand, heard Jesus' teaching for three solid years. He heard the same things often, and probably talked them over – indeed, argued about them – late into the night with Jesus and the other disciples. The words of Jesus soaked into him and became a part of the way he thought and hence remembered. So when he wrote his memoirs of Jesus' life, he was able to recall long speeches which Jesus had made, the minute details of incidents that he had witnessed, the tone of voice adopted by Jesus' opponents.

Scratching where people itch

But that doesn't account for all the differences between John and the other Gospels. Why are there so few incidents in John's account? Why are there no Synoptic-style parables? Why is the cleansing of the temple at the start and not at the end of Jesus' ministry?

We need to remind ourselves who John was writing for. His Gospel was for Jewish Christians who were under pressure to abandon their new-found faith in Christ and return to traditional Judaism. John wanted to show them clearly why such a course of action would be disastrous.

The way he did this was to show what Jesus did and said about the major festivals and institutions of the Jewish people. John wanted to show that it was Jesus who was now the focus of God's activity in the world and no longer the temple and feasts of the Jewish calendar.

This probably explains why the cleansing of the temple comes at the beginning of John's Gospel whereas it happens in the last week of Jesus' life according to Matthew, Mark and Luke. John could well have placed that story at the start of his account of Jesus' ministry as a kind of summary statement.   *(John 2:13–22)*

What he is saying is this: the Jesus you will meet in this Gospel is such an important figure in God's purposes for the world that he is replacing the temple. As we saw earlier, the temple stood at the heart of Jewish faith and practice. This also explains why John tells us that John the Baptist described Jesus as the 'Lamb of God who takes away the sin of the world'.

Elsewhere John shows us that Jesus often went up to Jerusalem to take part in the major festivals. For example, chapters 7 and 8 are set at the Feast of Tabernacles. This was the time when the people lived in tents on their roofs as a way of recalling the Israelites' journey through the wilderness after the Exodus. It was also a festival that looked forward to the day when God would send his Holy Spirit and establish his rule on earth.   *(John 7 – 8)*

This looking back and looking forward found its focus in a ceremony that happened every day of the seven days of the feast: the priests would draw water from the pool of Siloam, parade through the streets of Jerusalem with it and pour it over the altar in the temple. The water would stream out from the temple through the city, a visual aid reminding the people of how God had provided water in the desert and of how Ezekiel had seen a vision of living water streaming from the temple when the Kingdom of God had come in all its splendour and fulness.

It was on the last and greatest day of the feast, when

the water ceremony had happened for the seventh time, that Jesus said: 'Let anyone who is thirsty come to me and let the one who believes in me drink.' In this dramatic story John shows that Jesus was claiming to fulfil all the expectations of the Feast of Tabernacles. He was the one who would bring in the Kingdom of God. He was the one who would pour out the Holy Spirit on his people.   *(John 7:37–39)*

'Give us a sign'

To reinforce this key claim that Jesus is the focus of God's saving activity on earth, John has composed his account by putting together seven 'signs' – he doesn't call them miracles – surrounded by stories that throw light on what the signs tell us about Jesus.

They are: turning water into wine (2:1–11); healing the nobleman's son at Capernaum (4:46–54); healing the man

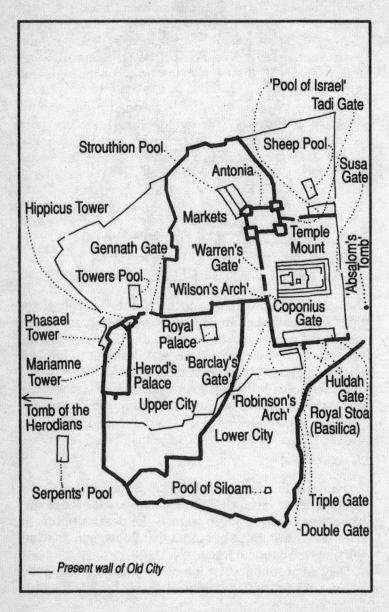

'Pool of Israel'
Tadi Gate
Strouthion Pool.
Sheep Pool.
Susa Gate
Antonia
Hippicus Tower
Markets
Temple Mount
Gennath Gate
'Warren's Gate'
'Absalom's Tomb'
Towers Pool
'Wilson's Arch'
Coponius Gate
Phasael Tower
Royal Palace
Mariamne Tower
Herod's Palace
'Barclay's Gate'
Huldah Gate
Tomb of the Herodians
Upper City
'Robinson's Arch'
Royal Stoa (Basilica)
Lower City
Serpents' Pool
Pool of Siloam...
Triple Gate
Double Gate

——— Present wall of Old City

at the pool (5:1–9); feeding the 5,000 (6:1–15); healing the blind man (9:1–8); raising Lazarus from death (11:1–44); and Jesus' own resurrection (20:1–29). The meaning of each of these signs is then explained by Jesus or John (with the possible exception of the changing of water into wine), with the focus being on what the signs tell us about Jesus.

All this is wrapped up in two ringing declarations about who Jesus is. The first is 1:1–14, where John recalls the creation of the world by God's Word and then tells us that that Word became flesh and lived with us. The second is Thomas' statement about Jesus a week after the resurrection: 'My Lord and my God.'   (John 20:28)

Keep the faith

John is a pastor. He loves the people God has put in his care. He wants to strengthen their faith and encourage them to stay loyal to its Founder. And so he has written a Gospel that warmly and compassionately shows us that Jesus is in fact God in the flesh, the One through whom we receive life and hope, grace and peace, the Kingdom of God and the Holy Spirit.

As he himself says about the purpose of his writing, 'These things are written so that you might continue to believe that Jesus is the Messiah, the Son of God, and that believing you may have life in his name.'

For further thought

Read John 6 – it's a long chapter but well worth the effort! It is John's account of the feeding of the 5,000 (see Matthew 14:13–21; Mark 6:32–44; Luke 9:10–17) and Jesus walking on the water (see Matthew 14:22–33; Mark 6:47–51).

Ask yourself these three questions:

(a) What do we learn about this incident from John that we don't learn from the Synoptics?

(b) What do we learn about Jesus from John's account that we don't learn from Matthew, Mark and Luke?

(c) Why do you think John told it the way he did?

CHAPTER 5

■■■■■■■■■

What Jesus did next

The Acts of the Apostles

*A*tlanta burns, the future's up for grabs and Rhet Butler turns to Scarlett and utters his immortal lines: 'Frankly, my dear, I don't give a damn'; the credits roll and the audience is left hanging.

Forty years later a publisher in America realized that a lot of people frankly did give a damn and wanted to know what happened to the hapless heroine of *Gone With the Wind*. So the publisher paid an author a million dollars to write the sequel.

Luke's Gospel ends with Jesus going up into heaven and the believers skipping back to Jerusalem full of beans and new life. But what happened then? What became of Peter, James, John and the others? What became of Jesus and his message?

Alone of the Gospel writers, Luke sets out to tell us in his unique second volume known to us as the Acts of the Apostles. This is not the most helpful title. Perhaps *What Jesus Did Next* would have been better.

Acts opens in Jerusalem and closes in Rome. On the

Making waves

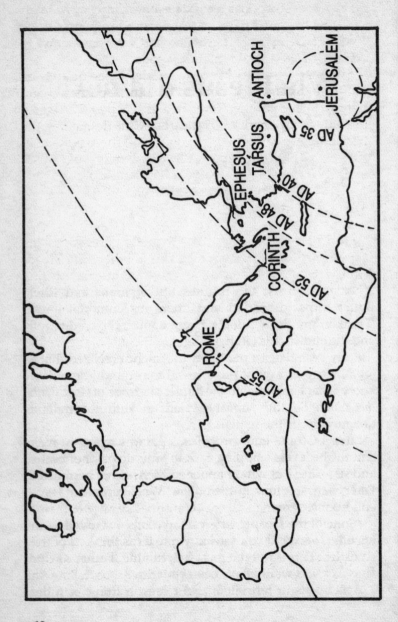

way it visits a lot of large cities between those capitals and a few smaller ones too. It tells how churches were set up, how the good news of Jesus spread to people of all kinds, classes and backgrounds and what happened to some of the key players in the Gospels.

But Acts is also a bit of a puzzle. Peter disappears half-way through and none of the other apostles except James, John's brother (executed in chapter 12), get a look-in. From chapter 9 onwards, Paul dominates the book. But even his story is unfinished. The last scene in Acts is of Paul awaiting trial, and we cry out, 'What happened next?' Luke never wrote volume three.

The edited highlights

One of the cornerstones of TV sports coverage is the edited highlights programme. This is where the broadcasters bring us not the whole game but just the exciting or important bits. If it's soccer, they show us the goals and the near-misses; if it's cricket, they show us the runs and wickets.

Well, Luke gives us the edited highlights of the history of the church from around AD 30 to the early 60s. But in order to read Acts right, we need to get a handle on why he selected the highlights he did and not others. What was it about the stories he tells us that attracted his attention?

If we can identify the point Luke was trying to make in writing Acts, we'll be a long way down the road of grasping why he wrote it as he did. And the best way to do that is to find out who he was writing for. What questions were they asking? How does he answer them?

Some have said that he was writing to show how the good news of Jesus spread from Jerusalem – a pretty obscure place – to every major city of the Empire, including Rome. After all, he begins with Jesus telling the Twelve to tell the world about him, starting in Judea, spreading out through Samaria and heading for the ends of the earth. And certainly the movement of people in Acts follows that pattern: starting in Jerusalem, moving out through Samaria, north to Antioch, Turkey, Greece and Rome. But while this could well have been part of Luke's purpose, it doesn't account for the way his book is put together.   *(Acts 1:8)*

Others suggest he was writing to reassure the Romans that the church was a peaceful religious movement and not a wild bunch of radicals hell-bent on overthrowing the state. After all, the founder of the church, Jesus of Nazareth, was crucified by the Roman government of Judea for challenging its power. And Paul, whose journey to Rome dominates the end of the book, had gone there to stand trial. This could explain why the outcome of the trial is unknown: Luke rushed this volume out as evidence of Paul's honourable conduct.

Acts, like Luke's Gospel, is dedicated to Theophilus, a wealthy Gentile who perhaps needed reassuring that he wasn't signing up to and funding a terrorist outfit. And it's true that the Roman authorities get a good press from Luke. The people who oppose the church and give the Christians a hard time in the courts are usually Jews and sometimes people involved in other religions whose livelihood is threatened by the arrival of Christianity – like the idol-makers in Ephesus.   *(Acts 1:1)*

But again, while Luke wanted to commend the good news of Jesus to the Roman authorities and to ensure that the church was not opposed for the wrong reasons, there's more to Acts than this.

Who can you trust these days?

Luke was clearly writing for an educated readership. He wasn't writing a popular paperback, but a work of literature. He was also, therefore, more than likely writing for city-dwellers, which explains why most of the action of

Acts takes place in cities. We hear virtually nothing of the church of Galilee – where the movement started, where Jesus lived and worked most of his life, where the bulk of the action in the Gospels happened – though we know from other sources that the church existed there in the villages and fishing communities from the earliest days. James's letter may well have been written to Christians there as well as to those in Judea and Samaria.

Luke was also a friend of Paul. They travelled together, preached the good news together, ate together and no doubt talked long into the night about what their message meant to the world they lived in. And especially how that message spoke to the great division in the world between Jew and Gentile. Paul was the Jew who had become an apostle to the Gentiles, and Luke was the Gentile who had thrown in his lot with an obscure Jewish sect; how did the good news of Jesus bring them together?   (Acts 16:11; Colossians 4:14)

When Paul tackled the issue he did so in his typical robust style in the letter to the Galatians, and then later, in more measured tones, when writing to the church at Ephesus. When Luke tackled it he did so in a story, just as he had done with the life and teaching of Jesus. Luke's story of the growth and spread of the church was written to show that God can be trusted: he keeps his promises and he fulfils his plans. How does Luke do this?

At the start of his Gospel Luke records the song of praise that Mary sang after the angel had visited her. In that song she told the world that God had kept his promise to Abraham. That promise was that the world would be saved through a child born to his family. That huge promise found its focus in Jesus on the cross bearing the punishment for the sins of the whole world.   (Luke 1:46–55; Genesis 12)

But the promise to Abraham could not be fulfilled if all that Jesus achieved was to found a renewal movement within first-century Judaism. The message of Jesus had to break out of the straitjacket of Jewish ethnic identity and embrace people of every race.

So Acts begins with Luke reminding Theophilus that in his first volume he had told his patron what Jesus *began* to do and teach, the implication being that this second volume would be a continuation of what Jesus came to do. But now that Jesus was in heaven, he would be working through his disciples, the church. Just as Jesus had been empowered for his task by the Holy Spirit, so now was the church. The Spirit came so that the church could take the good news to all the earth.

The church preached as Jesus had done. It also lived as he did, showing concern for the poor and marginalized, giving pride of place to praise and prayer, and being enabled by God to perform signs that demonstrated the truth of its message.

Having established that it is through the church that Jesus is continuing his work of bringing salvation to people through faith in him, Luke moves on to show how the church began to edge into the Gentile world. Luke stresses that on the day of Pentecost people from all over the world heard and received the message. But it's pretty clear that they were all practising Jews – whether born that way or having converted to Judaism from paganism.   *(Luke 2:5–12)*

The first move into the Gentile world came when God gave Peter a vision of animals that a good Jew wouldn't eat and invited him to dine. Peter saw the same vision three times – a conscious echo of his three-fold denial of Jesus. As soon as he had seen it, Gentiles called on Peter and he ate with them. The walls that divided Jew from Gentile were cracking. When God gave the Holy Spirit to Cornelius, the Gentile soldier, while Peter was explaining the message of Jesus, those walls came crashing to the ground – though it's clear from Galatians that Peter took a long time to come to terms with the shock of it.

From Pentecost to the fall of Jerusalem

AD

30

First Christian Pentecost

Stephen killed/
Paul converted

Philip in Samaria

Peter in
and out of prison

Cornelius, the Gentile,
converted

40

Paul in Antioch with
Barnabas

James, John's brother,
killed by Herod

Paul's first church-
planting tour

Famine

Paul's second church-
planting tour

Council in Jerusalem

50

Peter in Corinth

Paul's third church-
planting tour

Paul arrested in Jerusalem

Paul arrives in Rome

Peter in Rome

60

Great fire sparks off
persecution of Christians by
Nero

Paul and Peter executed

Jewish rebellion

Jerusalem falls/
temple destroyed

70

73

(Acts 10:9–23; Galatians 2:11–14; Acts 10:23–48)

The stoning of Stephen in Jerusalem had been followed by a great persecution against the church there, and believers fleeing from it had preached, chattered and shared the gospel all the way up the coast to Antioch, where Gentiles came to faith in Jesus and believers were called Christians for the first time. No longer was the church just a sect within Judaism: it was breaking out and taking on a separate identity of its own.

That process was very painful. Luke records the debate that took place in Jerusalem between those who wanted to welcome the Gentiles with open arms and those who were insisting that the Gentiles become Jews before they became Christians. The so-called Jerusalem Council decreed that nothing should be put in the way of Gentiles coming to faith in Christ. The fact was that God had shown that this was his will by giving the gift of the Holy Spirit to the Gentiles in almost the same way as he had given it to the original Jewish believers on the day of Pentecost.   *(Acts 15:1–29)*

Caterpillars become butterflies

After the Council, Luke's focus of attention shifts north to Antioch, the base for Paul's mission, and further afield as the good news of Jesus was enthusiastically received by Gentiles all over the Empire. Indeed, while the Gentiles were flocking to hear and believe the gospel of a crucified Jewish healer and teacher, the Jews were getting decidedly frosty. Paul was hounded around the Near East by Jews seeking to have him silenced. And sadly, some Jewish Christians joined in.   *(Acts 17:1–9)*

But it seems the more he was opposed, the more Paul's mission saw success among the Gentiles, with churches being planted in many major cities between Antioch and Rome. Luke, it seems, is telling us in story form what Paul himself tells us in Romans 9 – 11; that God is using the mystery of Jewish unbelief to open his Kingdom to the Gentiles and so fulfil his promise to Abraham.

It wasn't that God had abandoned one lot of people, the Jews, and taken up with a new crowd, the Gentiles – that would hardly suggest that God is someone you can rely on. Rather, God was creating a new people out of his old people, much as a butterfly is created out of a caterpillar. His new people consisted of both Jews and Gentiles, united not by their ethnic origin, but by their faith in Christ and their sharing of the life of God through the Holy Spirit living within and among them.

Getting the point

'So you see, from Acts 2 it is clear that everyone must be baptized in the Spirit after they have been converted,' he said.

'Ah, but what about the conversion of Cornelius? He was baptized in the Holy Spirit before he repented or acknowledged Jesus as Lord,' she replied.

'Acts 6 clearly shows that churches should be run by deacons elected by the church members,' she asserted.

'Wait a minute,' he replied. 'Acts 14 and 19 clearly show that churches should be governed by elders appointed by apostles who are responsible for a number of churches.'

There's nothing quite like the Acts of the Apostles for causing disagreement among believers from different church traditions! The fact is that each of the statements above is based on an episode in Acts, but none of them is true.

Acts 2 is the story of a unique event – the first coming of the Holy Spirit on the church. It is not the pattern for conversion. Neither is the story of Cornelius, the first Gentile believer. Acts 6 has nothing at all to do with deacons in the modern Baptist or Free Church use of that title, and Acts 14 and 19 aren't much of a guide for contemporary house churches.

The point is that Luke didn't write Acts to tell us how the church was organized. He isn't very interested in the nitty-gritty, day-to-day running of the church. He certainly isn't laying down a pattern that must be followed by Christians in every age.

The Seven appointed in Acts 6, for instance, are never called deacons and exercise most of their ministry away from the Jerusalem church that appointed them. Luke never tells us how or why James, Jesus' brother (who hadn't believed in Jesus prior to the crucifixion) came to be the leader of the church in Jerusalem. He doesn't tell us that every church established by Paul was run the same way.

People who come to Acts because they want to find out how to get back to the New Testament church are in for a disappointment. There just isn't enough information. Luke's intention is for us to see what happened and who was behind it. God was gathering his people, in accordance with his promise to Abraham, from the Jewish world and the Gentile world. The agent he was using was the church, and the means was the preaching of the good news of Jesus, inspired by the Holy Spirit, who also demonstrated the truth of the message in people's lives.

If Acts contains a model or pattern for us to follow it is this: the church in every generation exists to proclaim the gospel of Jesus Christ. If it does that, it will be inspired and led by the Spirit of Jesus operating in the lives of believers, bringing unbelievers to an awareness of the truth of the gospel. As to organization and methods, Luke's message is this: whatever works to achieve this goal and is in line with the message and the Spirit of Jesus is OK.

For further thought

Acts is a record of how the church spread around the ancient world. Then, as now, the church ran into problems. Read Acts 6:1–7; 11:1–18; 15:1–35. What do we learn about:

(a) how to resolve conflicts between believers?

(b) how the church can deal with racism in its own structures and thus be a beacon to the world on this sensitive, vital issue?

CHAPTER 6

■■■■■■■■■

The second founder

The life and times of Paul the apostle

■■■■■■■

*I*n the sharp sunlight, he was standing guard over a pile of coats, sternly nodding his approval. A group of men, their faces masked by shadows from the nearby city wall, were hurling stones, boulders, or any lump of masonry they could lift at the bleeding form of a man dying out in the merciless heat.

The group finished their bloody toil, gathered their coats and melted away into the hustle of the city streets. Their anger spent on the church's first martyr, Stephen, they went back to their daily routines.   *(Acts 7:54 – 8:1)*

But, for Saul, the young rabbi who had guarded their coats, it was only the beginning. If Stephen could be removed, then so could all the other 'heretics', all those who preached that Jesus from Nazareth, a trouble-maker crucified a couple of years before, was God's Messiah.

A few days later, having set off from Jerusalem to Damascus on a mission to destroy the church there, Saul was preaching that Jesus was the Son of God. So powerful was his preaching, so radical the change in him, so

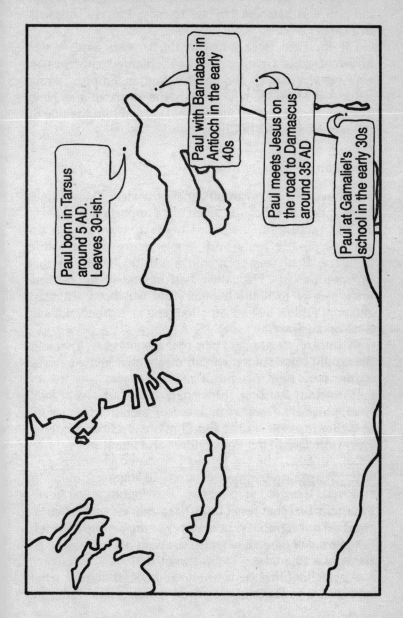

effective his call to Jews to believe in Jesus, that a plot to kill him was hatched. He had to escape from Damascus in a basket.

For the next twenty-five to thirty years Saul, better known by his Greek name Paul, planted churches in every major city of the eastern Roman Empire, wrote letters, thirteen of which form the heart of the New Testament and had an impact that earned him the title of the second founder of Christianity.

The man for the Gentiles

Paul once told a Roman officer at Jerusalem, 'I am a Jew, from Tarsus in Cilicia, a citizen of an important city' (Acts 21:39). Tarsus, on the Turkish coast, was on a main east–west trade route and was a centre of the textile industry. Paul was born into a wealthy family in this prosperous city. His father had obviously done some great service to Rome because Paul was born a Roman citizen. Perhaps he had supplied tents or leather goods to the Roman army.

Citizenship made Paul part of the social elite. That and his family's undoubted wealth meant that he had access to the very best in education. Tarsus was a centre of culture and learning, philosophy and art. And Paul clearly made the most of it, as can be seen from his ability to write, to argue a case and to quote freely and extensively from Greek and Roman ideas and literature.

A man with a mission

Paul told the Philippian Christians that he was 'circumcised on the eighth day, a member of the people of Israel, of the tribe of Benjamin, a Hebrew born of Hebrews; as to the Law, a Pharisee'.   *(Philippians 3:5)*

For all his wealth, learning and social status, what mattered most to Paul was that he was a Jew. He came from a strict Jewish home, where Aramaic was probably spoken. He would have attended the local synagogue school, where he would have been tutored in the Law and the tradition of his people. Then he went to Jerusalem to finish his education. Going to Jerusalem was pretty impressive for a boy from the Diaspora, but to sit at the feet of the great Gamaliel was something else. Paul got the very best Jewish education that money and connections could secure.   *(Acts 22:3)*

But he was always more than just a well-educated rabbi. He had fire in his belly. From his career in Acts and the tone and content of his letters, it is clear that Paul was no ivory-tower theologian, no bookish academic. He was passionate about everything he did; he did it all for a purpose and saw himself as a man with a mission.

This commitment and drive are seen before his conversion to Christianity. While still a pupil (though probably nearing the end of his studies, which makes him around thirty years old), he began to oppose the young church. He did not just engage the Christians in debate – he wanted to snuff out the movement. Hence his role in Stephen's martyrdom.

Here we see the difference between Paul and his distinguished teacher. Gamaliel clearly wanted to reserve judgment on Christianity. When the apostles were arrested and brought before the court in Jerusalem, it was Gamaliel who counselled caution, saying that if the movement was the work of men it would fail, as other such movements had before it, but if it was a move of God within Judaism, the leaders of the Jews would not be able to stop it; worse, to try to stop it would be tantamount to fighting God.

Gamaliel's wait-and-see wisdom prevailed, and the apostles were released. But Paul wasn't so patient. The new heresy had to be stamped out. God needed a helping hand, and Paul was just the man to offer it.

Having seen off Stephen and having helped spark off widespread persecution of the church in Jerusalem, he played a prominent part in arresting known Christians.

So effective was his assault on the believers that many of them fled the city. Paul, scenting victory, and having clearly caught the public mood, was empowered by the priests in Jerusalem to spread the net wider. He set off to Damascus, pledged to weed out the Christians before the church could take root there.

Blinded by the light

In the heat and dust of the Damascus road Paul ran into the person he was least expecting – Jesus. The meeting rocked Paul to the core, shattered his old understanding of God and the world, and planted the seeds that blossomed into his radical gospel of freedom. *(Acts 9:1–19)*

Within sight of the walls of Damascus, Paul met the living Jesus. So Jesus wasn't the rightly crucified messianic pretender that Paul had thought. If God had raised him from the dead, then his claim to be the bringer of the Kingdom, the source of new life, the one who would give the Holy Spirit to his followers, must be true.

But there was more. If Jesus was the Messiah and he had ended up on a cross, that can't have been an accident. God would not have allowed his plans for his Messiah to be thwarted by chance. So the cross must have been central to Jesus' work as the Messiah.

And surely there was still more. The glorious appearance of Jesus on the road was very like the glorious appearance of God when he showed himself to people in Old Testament times. What did this tell Paul – blinded by that light, his mind sent into a whirl of speculation – about who and what Jesus was?

And finally, why did Jesus say Paul was persecuting

him, when he was in fact persecuting the church? What did this begin to teach Paul about the nature of the church as the body of Christ on earth?

All these questions and implications arose from Paul's encounter with Jesus on the road. But, as ever with Paul, he did not withdraw for the luxury of several months' quiet reflection on these issues while he got together a perfect systematic theology with which he could wow the world. Paul hardly paused to catch his breath.

This little light of mine

He was led into Damascus, helpless and blind. He was met by Ananias – who was none too pleased at the prospect and took some persuading from God before he went. He baptized Paul and welcomed him into the fellowship of the church. The rather stunned believers met the new convert and listened to him powerfully proclaiming the risen Jesus to Jews in the city. This latter activity (which could well have lasted up to three years, depending on how we relate Acts 9 to Galatians 1) did not go down well with Paul's former supporters. They plotted his death and he had to escape.   *(Acts 9:19–22)*

He came to Jerusalem at around this time and met the apostles who were still there. It has to be said that they were suspicious of him, but Barnabas took him under his wing, introduced him to everyone and gave him the opportunity to preach and teach. The situation in Jerusalem was delicate, and Paul's style stirred up vicious opposition among the religious and political authorities. It was time to move on again.

Paul left Jerusalem for Tarsus, his home town. We know nothing of his stay there, though it is probably fair to speculate that he would have had some difficulty explaining his conversion to his family. Life would not have been easy for this promising son who kicked over the traces and threw in his lot with a new and, in the eyes

Paul's journeys

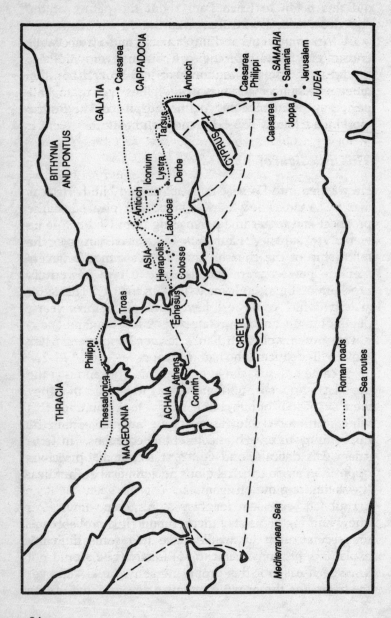

of his father and his former teachers, dangerously heretical sect.

Barnabas came and found him some time later and took him to a new church in Antioch, mid-way between Tarsus and Damascus. Jewish Christians who had been scattered by the persecution that had broken out after Stephen was martyred had worked their way up to Antioch, the commercial and political capital of the Roman province of Syria. They preached wherever they went to whoever would listen, and for the first time Gentiles came into the church.   (Acts 11:25–26)

This mixed church needed teaching and setting on a firm foundation. Barnabas could think of no better colleague for this work than Paul, the one Jesus had called to be his messenger to the Gentiles.

From Antioch Paul and Barnabas went to Jerusalem for a crucial meeting of the apostles to talk about evangelism among the Gentiles. Paul seems to have been fairly pleased with the outcome: that Gentiles didn't have to become Jews to become Christians! He went home to Antioch and from there launched out on his three major expeditions that took him to virtually every big city of the eastern half of the Roman Empire.

Have mission, will travel

For much of the next ten years he travelled, preaching the good news of Jesus and planting churches. He never travelled alone. From his letters it is clear that there was always a team around him. Sometimes, if Paul was staying a long time in one place (*e.g.* he spent eighteen months at Ephesus), members of his team would go to the outlying towns and villages and preach the gospel there. For example, while Paul was at Ephesus, Epaphras planted the church at Colosse just down the valley.
(Acts 19:1–10)

As well as preaching, Paul also raised funds, not for

himself but for the poor in the church at Jerusalem and in Judea. Through the 40s and 50s, life in Israel was bleak. Famine and economic hardship meant that many Christians had virtually nothing to live on. Paul could not stand by and do nothing about this tragedy.

So he appealed to the Gentile churches he had founded – and to some he hadn't – to help relieve the poverty of the Jewish congregations in Palestine. As well as bringing practical aid to the suffering Christians, Paul also believed that this would demonstrate the unity of the church and the reality of the fellowship of believers in Christ. And furthermore, he felt that this offering by Gentile Christians would somehow demonstrate the truth of the gospel to his own people, the Jews. It is this collection that Paul is talking about in 1 Corinthians 16:1–4 and 2 Corinthians 9.

In around 57 he brought the collection to Jerusalem. He had been warned that his journey would be dangerous, but he wanted to bring the offering personally. Having done so, he was arrested in the temple and brought before the council. They wanted to execute him but couldn't without Roman approval, and because Paul was a Roman citizen he couldn't be treated in the summary way that Jesus was.   *(Acts 21:17)*

The Roman governor, warned that certain people, with the approval of the priests, were planning to kill Paul on his next public appearance, had him moved under armed guard to Caesarea to the safe-keeping of Governor Felix. He couldn't decide what to do with the troublesome missionary, and Paul remained in prison for two years.

Felix was replaced by Festus, and he, keen to curry favour with the Jewish leaders in Jerusalem, wanted to send Paul back there for trial. So Paul appealed to Caesar, as it was the right of every Roman citizen to be tried personally by the Emperor. After a hazardous and eventful journey, Paul arrived in Rome, and there he remained for two years, able to preach and teach and receive visitors, awaiting his trial.   *(Acts 25:1–12)*

A final spurt

This much we know from Acts. But that's where Luke leaves off. And we aren't sure what happened next. But it seems likely that sometime after the end of Acts, Paul was released. He travelled again, probably to Spain, as he had told the Roman church he wanted to. He then probably went back to Corinth, which served as the hub for a new work around Turkey and the Aegean. It was during this time that Paul wrote 1 Timothy and Titus.

It is quite likely that he was there for two years or so, from about 64 to 66. Towards the end of this time, the church in Rome began to suffer appallingly at the hands of Nero. Peter had probably already died at the hands of this madman. At great personal risk, Paul went to Rome in about 66 or 67 to strengthen and encourage the Roman Christians. There he met his death after composing a last, poignant letter to his dear friend and colleague Timothy.

For further thought

In Acts 22:3 – 23:11 Paul is telling his story – how he came to faith in Jesus, how he has lived since – to a variety of people. His story is not only about him, it is also a way of telling the crowd the good news about Jesus. Write out your story – how you came to faith, how you live your life now as a Christian – in a way that would commend the gospel to someone who does not yet believe.

CHAPTER 7

■ ■ ■ ■ ■ ■ ■ ■ ■

Words on the run

Paul's letters to churches and friends

---

*W*hen I was a young Christian I was asked to give my testimony at a school meeting. I was scared witless! But I was encouraged by a letter from Dave Pope. At that time he was an evangelist with the Movement for World Evangelisation and was about to release his first album. He and I had never met – he knew about me through one of his colleagues.

He wrote that he was thrilled to hear that I'd become a Christian and was about to tell others what Jesus meant to me. He assured me that God would give me the courage I needed to take this step and that he'd be praying for me. I was knocked for six. It was such an encouragement that someone like Dave Pope should take an interest in me. Letters can give people's faith such a boost. Perhaps the Christians in Philippi and Thessalonica felt that way when a letter from Paul arrived.

But there are also other kinds of letters that we're not so keen to receive. I got a letter once from a couple involved in youth work at the church I was attending at the time, telling me how hurt they had been by something I had done. The letter warned me that our friendship was at risk if I didn't do something. I felt a mixture of anger and sorrow, but I knew I had to act. The issue between us was resolved, I was forgiven, and our relationship was restored. I guess I felt a bit of what the Corinthian Christians must have felt during their correspondence with Paul – a correspondence which was long and painful, but which, it seems, ultimately resulted in restored relationships.

Before the age of the telephone and the fax, letters were the essential means of keeping in touch, passing on messages, warning of dangers and seeking reconciliation between people who had fallen out. We see all of this in Paul's letters.

'Quick, Silvanus, take a letter'

Today when the major issues of politics or faith are being debated or promoted, people write books, essays, articles in learned journals and pamphlets. Paul wrote letters. Some people suggest that if Paul was around today he would probably write books – if a publisher could tie him down long enough to meet a deadline! But Paul did live at a time when people wrote books.

At Alexandria in Egypt there lived a devout Jew who committed his life to proving to the Gentile world that the Jewish understanding of things was the right one. His name was Philo and he wrote books – books with a beginning, a middle and an end, books with a line of argument that could be followed quite easily by anyone picking them up. Paul, however, chose to write letters.

He had been called by God to preach the good news of Jesus to the Gentiles, and he did this by planting churches in key urban centres. Having started a church, he would stay a while to ensure that the church's foundations were strong and that leaders were in place, and

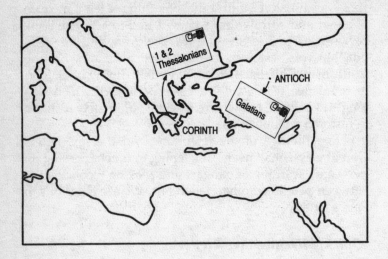

then he would move on. He kept in touch with the churches he founded by making visits and by writing letters.

The nature of Paul's life meant that he wrote only when he heard of a major problem in a church (*e.g.* Galatians, 1 and 2 Corinthians); or when he was in prison (*e.g.* Philippians), the forced leisure time being put to good pastoral use; or when he was asked questions (1 Corinthians, 1 Thessalonians). He frequently had to defend himself against attacks made on his character or ministry by other 'apostles' (1 and 2 Corinthians, 1 Thessalonians). He also wrote to individual members of his ministry team who had been given a specific job to do. He wrote to encourage them – as Dave Pope did to me – and to remind them of what they should be doing (1 and 2 Timothy, Titus).

Paul's letters were always provoked by something happening in the church he was writing to. He never seems to have sat down and said to himself: 'I know, I'll drop a line to the church at Damascus, telling them all about the doctrine of justification by faith.' He wrote in response to a crisis or false teaching or some situation that might affect the long-term health of the church in question.

So, reading Paul's letters is a bit like hearing one end of a phone conversation. We rarely know what the specific event was that provoked Paul to put pen to parchment – or to get his secretary to take a letter. We have to try to work it out from what he said.

Paul's teaching comes to us, not in a systematic and carefully ordered way, but as arguments used to persuade his readers that he and not his opponents had the right understanding of the Christian faith.

The view from the battlefield

So Paul was no ivory-tower theologian watching the world and the church from the wings, but a working minister and evangelist who lived in the thick of the battle to establish the church of Jesus Christ.

But his letters are not random jottings or haphazard missives fired off in a rush between engagements. He wrote with care, and there is a sharp and creative mind behind what he wrote, even though the occasion for each of his letters was a problem in or a request from a church. The letters exploded out of his rich intellect and fertile imagination. To understand the letters, you need to understand the man and his sense of calling.

Paul was first and foremost a pastor. He cared deeply and passionately for the people he had led to the Lord and the churches he had founded. He was anxious when he heard of congregations being troubled by persecution, divisions or false teaching. *(Colossians 2:1–2)*

So, sometimes he wrote to answer specific questions

raised by churches (1 Corinthians, 1 Thessalonians); sometimes because he had heard of serious problems in a church from a close friend or colleague (Colossians, Galatians); and sometimes because he knew that a friend needed encouragement (1 Timothy).

Paul is often seen as a cold, fierce, rigid dogmatist. But this is an awful caricature. He sometimes pastored in anger, but usually he spoke with great gentleness. We see this in his fatherly concern for the Thessalonians, his anguish over Titus' health, his yearning to see Philemon and Onesimus reconciled, his longing for companionship when he faced danger. His great heart for people is seen in the long list of greetings in Romans 16.

Secondly, Paul was a teacher. His message was derived from Jesus Christ himself, whom he had met on the road to Damascus, and from the teaching of the church handed down from the very beginning. He taught this truth winsomely, with great conviction, angrily and gently (compare and contrast two early letters written within a couple of years of each other: Galatians and 1 Thessalonians).

His teaching had two major purposes. The first was to refute false teaching and to correct misunderstandings which people had. When he heard that Christians in Galatia were getting circumcised and were trying to keep the Jewish Law, he wrote furiously denouncing the people who were laying such burdens on the young believers and passionately defending his gospel of faith and freedom.   (*Galatians 3:1; Colossians 2:4*)

His teaching in 1 Corinthians 12 –14 is not a measured summary of everything there is to know about spiritual gifts but an attempt to correct false views about the importance of tongues and to prevent the Corinthians' worship from descending into chaos.

His second purpose was to remind people of the central truths of the faith, and especially that they must live the Christian life in a way that shows the world that the gospel is true. So he stresses that people can be right with God only through faith in Jesus. But, once put right, their lives should be marked by good works, kind words and a lifestyle that honours God.

Building on the past

Thirdly, Paul was a Pharisee. This meant that his whole way of thinking had been shaped by the Old Testament and the teaching of the synagogue. When he met Jesus on the road to Damascus he didn't ditch this rich heritage – he wasn't spirited away from his past. He wrestled with how to interpret his Bible (the Old Testament) in the light of his experience of meeting the risen Jesus. And so his teaching is rooted in the Scriptures he had grown up with. *(Philippians 3:4–5)*

Paul's letters: the busy 50s

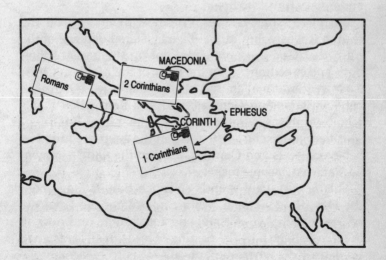

As he studied and prayed he saw that God had always accepted people on the basis of their faith, and that the things that marked the Jews out from the world – circumcision, the Sabbath, certain rules regarding what you eat and how you eat it – were fine in their day as an outward expression of that faith. But now they had been superseded by Christ and the coming of the Holy Spirit. What marked out the people of God now was not these so-called 'works of the Law' but the fruit of the Holy Spirit, made possible by faith in Christ.

So Paul frequently refers to and quotes from the Old Testament. When he does so, he shows how a particular passage is fulfilled in Jesus, and how it now applies to those who are members of God's people through faith in Jesus.   *(1 Corinthians 10:6)*

His passion for the Old Testament is seen most clearly in his letter to the church at Rome. It was written during a three-month pause in around AD 56, and many see it as his finest work. Many also suggest that Romans is less a letter and more a treatise, a summation of his gospel – possibly written to elicit Rome's support for his proposed missionary travels to Spain.

But even Romans was written with an eye on the church it was going to. Paul's magisterial defence of the truth that God accepts people not on the basis of their birth and breeding but on the basis of their faith in Christ was written to a church where there were tensions between Jews and Gentiles, and at a time when Paul's whole emphasis was under attack from other Christians – so-called 'Judaisers' – who felt that the gospel required all believers, Jews and Gentiles, to keep the Old Testament Law at least in some respects.

This is why Paul spends so much time talking about the Day of Atonement, Abraham, Adam, the Law, the relationship between Israel and the church, and how all these are affected by the coming of Jesus. It all leads up to Romans 15:7, where he appeals to us to 'welcome one

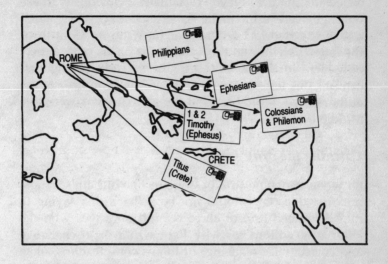

another, therefore, just as Christ has welcomed you, for the glory of God'.

'Do as I say and as I do'

Finally, Paul wrote as an apostle. As the opening of Galatians makes abundantly clear, Paul had no doubts about his calling or his gospel: both came straight from God. In 1 Corinthians he stresses that what he teaches is inspired by the Spirit and should be obeyed. He is so certain that the message upon which he has based his life and ministry is the whole truth, that he can appeal to his readers to copy his lifestyle; if they do that they'll be copying Christ. *(1 Corinthians 11:1)*

In anyone else this would have been appalling arrogance. Yet even in his lifetime others sensed that some of what Paul wrote was special in the way the Old

Testament Scriptures were special. Not everything, though. Paul wrote more than the thirteen letters collected in the New Testament. Obviously these writings were seen to be especially touched by God, unlike the two lost letters that he wrote to Corinth or the letter he wrote to the Laodiceans or his other letters of which we know nothing. By the end of the first century, his letters were being used as Scripture, as the authoritative Word of God in churches all over the Middle East.

Catching the drift

So when we come to a passage in one of Paul's letters, our first question should not be 'What's this saying to me?' We need first of all to remind ourselves who the letter was written to, why Paul wrote it (to challenge and correct false teaching, or to answer questions, or to give more detail to teaching already touched on?), and where the passage we're reading comes in the flow of his argument. We need to note whether he is quoting the Old Testament, and if so, what he's quoting and how he's using it.

So, taking Colossians 2:6–15 as an example, how does this work? This passage urges us to stay rooted in Christ (verses 6–7), to resist the world (verse 8) and to receive the fulness which is found only in Jesus (verses 9–15). The language Paul uses is rather odd, however: he talks of fulness, refers (apparently out of the blue) to circumcision and baptism, and mentions spiritual powers and authorities. This should alert us to the fact that Paul was probably countering some kind of false teaching that emphasized these things.   (*Colossians 2:6–15*)

Sure enough, a little background reading reveals that the Colossian church was troubled by teachers who talked a lot about needing to add new experiences to our faith in Jesus in order to receive the fulness of God in our lives. These teachers stressed the need to acquire secret knowledge – things that ordinary Christians didn't know – if you wanted to be especially spiritual. They said that it was necessary to go through secret initiation rituals to get a leg up on to a higher plane of Christian living.

Paul counters this teaching by stressing that the fulness of God is found only in Jesus. He had gone into detail about this in Colossians 1, where he had composed or quoted a wonderful poetic hymn of praise to Christ, the church's Lord, the visible image of the unseen God (verses 15–20).

He goes on to say that we experience the fulness of God through faith in Christ's death on the cross. It is his death on our behalf that has dealt with our sin and with all the oppressive powers – human and divine – that would prevent us from enjoying the fulness of life that God wants us to have.

Far from needing to undergo some secret ritual, by being baptized in public we have already testified to our faith in Jesus and to all the things which that faith has opened up to us. That's all we need, says Paul, because the way to fulness of life is through faith in Jesus, not secret knowledge and flashy new experiences, however wonderful and plausible they sound.

We need to do this kind of exercise every time we read a passage in one of Paul's letters. In this way we will catch his drift and not get caught in some whirlpool of misunderstanding that does no justice to Paul and nothing to build up our faith.

For further thought

Read 1 Corinthians 1:4–9; Ephesians 1:15–23; Philippians 1:3–11; and Colossians 1:3–12. These are reports of what Paul has been praying about.

(a) What do we learn from these passages about what mattered to Paul?

(b) If you were writing a report on what you pray about for your church, what would it contain?

CHAPTER 8

■■■■■■■■■

From our own correspondents

James, Peter, Jude and Hebrews

━━━━━━

*F*or years BBC Radio 4 has run a twice-weekly show giving its reporters from around the world the chance to bring us news from places not normally addressed in the main bulletins. *From Our Own Correspondent* is refreshing and informative. It shows us that important things are happening outside the capitals of the rich nations. It highlights events that are not focused on the politicians. It rounds out our picture of the world.

When we read the New Testament, our attention is so often concentrated on Paul's letters and the Gospels that we miss the news from other correspondents who bring fresh insights and new light to bear on the Christian landscape. The New Testament rounds out our picture of the Christian world by including writings from John (see the next two chapters), James, Peter, Jude and the author of Hebrews. The last four writers are unique, perceptive voices from the front line who deserve more of a hearing than they seem to get in our churches these days.

A voice from Jerusalem

There are three people in the New Testament called James. But only James the brother of Jesus can have written the letter that bears his name. John's brother died too early (around AD 44), and the other James – the son of Alphaeus, one of the Twelve – is too obscure to have written it without more clearly identifying himself.

James was the leader of the Jerusalem church from the mid-40s. After Peter escaped Herod's clutches, he never returned to Jerusalem, leaving James to take up the reins. The Lord's brother was certainly the leading man by the time of the Jerusalem Council, which was called in around 48 or 49 to settle the issue of what to do with the Gentiles who were flocking into the church.   *(Acts 15:12)*

At that council James showed himself to be a skilful diplomat, a peacemaker and someone keen to preserve both the purity and the evangelistic cutting edge of the church. He probably wrote the letter containing the decision of the council that was sent to Antioch. There are notable similarities of language between that letter and the one that bears his name in the New Testament.   *(Acts 15:23–29)*

It is entirely possible that the letter of James comes from around this time, maybe a few months before the council met. There is a view that suggests the letter, at least in the form in which we have it in our Bibles, is much later – as late as the 80s. But this is unlikely, for the following reasons.

There is no reference to the fall of Jerusalem in the letter. There is no evidence of any dispute between Jews and Gentiles in the church, suggesting that it comes from a time before the events that led to the Jerusalem Council. The Jewish tone of the letter suggests that it comes from a time when the Christians still viewed themselves as a movement within Judaism. The recipients appear to be recent converts, and the organization of the church appears to be pretty rudimentary, suggesting an early date.

If it does come from the late 40s, it was written at a crucial time. Firstly, it comes from the time after the martyrdom of Stephen and the scattering of Christians that happened in the wake of that, but before the controversy over Gentiles that led to the Jerusalem Council. The dispersion of Christians who chattered and gossiped the gospel wherever they went meant that new churches were springing up all over Palestine without apostolic leadership. The letter appears to be a collection of sermons geared towards grounding new Christians in their faith. It could well have been a written form of James's nurture-group Bible study material.

Secondly, the letter was written at a time of economic hardship – hence the amount of space devoted in James's teaching to the vital subject of wealth and possessions. Famine came to the whole region between 45 and 47. The majority of his audience would have been rural labourers and peasant farmers – though some probably lived in the coastal trading towns and were business people – and hence they were finding it hard to make ends meet.

In the political instability fostered by recession and famine, landowners forced down wages and seized the land of these smallholders, who were unable to keep up with their rents. This led to growing discontent that strengthened support among the poor for radical groups like the Zealots. James led a church that gave a high priority to sharing and ensuring that no-one was in need. He was clearly concerned to see the same spirit of sharing and generosity in all these new churches springing up around the Palestinian countryside.   (James 5:1–6)

But as well as teaching on wealth and possessions, James covers a number of other basic, vital teachings of the kind needed by new Christians. He tells them to expect suffering and how to handle it when it comes; he teaches about the need to be people who pray; he stresses that genuine faith will lead to works of love and charity; and he speaks of a Christian lifestyle that is marked by submission to God, sincerity and simplicity. Much of what he says is based on the Sermon on the Mount, as recorded by Matthew in his Gospel, which suggests that James had access to the same collection of teaching; he was, of course, writing some time before Matthew completed his Gospel.

The view from the rock

Having left Jerusalem because Herod was baying for his blood, Peter headed north. He certainly went to Antioch and probably to Corinth, though how long he stayed in either place is anyone's guess. He must have spent a significant period of time in Asia Minor (what is now Turkey), since it is to Christians in that region that his first and most substantial letter is addressed. Then he went to Rome.

There is a tradition that Paul asked him to come to Rome to help sort out growing divisions in the church, but there is no way of knowing whether there's any truth in this. It is, however, almost certain that Peter was in Rome in the early 60s and that he died there, along with Paul, in the sudden explosion of hostility against Christians which was set off by Nero in 64 following the great fire and which lasted until that Emperor's death in 68.

We know he was in Rome when he wrote his letters, because his first letter clearly shows that he was there: 'Your sister church in Babylon, chosen together with you, sends you greetings, and so does my son Mark.' Babylon was a code word for Rome commonly used by Christians, especially in times of persecution. John refers to Rome as Babylon in the book of Revelation.   *(1 Peter 5:13)*

It seems likely that persecution was in the air when Peter wrote his first letter. The state still seems basically good but there are suggestions of Christians being slandered and taken before magistrates to account for their beliefs. Peter encourages his readers to stand firm and follow the example of Jesus, whom he likens to Isaiah's suffering servant, an innocent victim who bore unjust suffering and maintained his faith in God. *(1 Peter 2:13–14)*

Peter's first letter is very carefully put together and beautifully written in the Greek of an educated and cultured man. This has given rise to the suggestion that a Galilean fisherman couldn't possibly have written it. But this is unfair. John Bunyan was a barely educated Bedford tinker, yet the English of *Pilgrim's Progress* is a joy to read. Joseph Conrad was a Polish seaman whose second language was French and who began learning English only at the age of twenty-one, yet he wrote some of the most evocative and flawless prose of twentieth-century English fiction.

So, Peter's Greek was probably better than we'd expect from a Palestinian. It also needs to be borne in mind that Silvanus, who delivered the letter, probably took it down in writing as Peter dictated it to him. Any wrinkles in Peter's Greek could well have been ironed out by him.

The careful construction of the letter has also given rise to suggestions that it is not a letter at all but a sermon, possibly even one preached at a baptismal service. The text certainly deals with many aspects of the Christian life that would be appropriate to a baptismal candidate. Perhaps what we have here is an edited form of the teaching for Peter's baptismal preparation classes. Whatever the letter's precise form, Peter is clear about its purpose: 'I have written this short letter to encourage you and to testify that this is the true grace of God. Stand fast in it.' *(1 Peter 5:12)*

A close circle of friends

According to Paul, Peter was accompanied on his travels by 'the Lord's brother'. In all likelihood he means Jude, since James was certainly in Jerusalem all this time. Jude is author of the last and probably most obscure letter in the New Testament. He possibly also had a hand in the second letter sent out under Peter's name. Certainly, most of Jude's letter is in 2 Peter. So it is possible that Jude, as Peter's close colleague and assistant, adapted his earlier writing, expanded it with new information and teaching from Peter and sent it to the same group of churches in Turkey. Or perhaps Jude took 2 Peter, edited it down, focused it more on false teaching and sent it out under his own name a few months after the apostle's second letter.

Two issues seem to have provoked both letters. The first was the threat that false teachers were posing to the churches that Peter and Jude had worked with in Turkey. Both letters contain dire warnings about the consequences of perverting the truth of the gospel. The second issue was the fact that persecution was hotting up. Being a Christian was risky. Even talking openly about the faith among themselves was becoming harder as the authorities began to crack down on what they saw as a potentially troublesome sect.   (Jude 3–4)

So Jude and 2 Peter contain language and images drawn from Jewish apocalyptic writings. These were the fantasy best-sellers of the first century. They told the story of God and the world in a way similar to that used in C. S. Lewis's *Narnia Chronicles* or Stephen Lawhead's *Albion* trilogy.   (Jude 9, 14)

The Jews started writing apocalypses when it was dangerous for them to speak openly about their faith. So they are written in a kind of code. If you know how the code works, you can understand what the writing is saying. If you don't, then it just appears to be a pretty or

The correspondents

Peter and Philip travelling in Judea and Samaria

Peter leaves Judea for good

Herod dies

James writes to churches in Palestine, Syria and beyond

Peter in Corinth?

Peter in Rome

Great fire in Rome sparks off persecution of church

Hebrews written possibly from Ephesus or Antioch probably to Jewish Christians in Rome

AD
35

40

45

50

55

60

65

70

James, John's brother, executed by Herod

Famine in Palestine and Syria

Peter in Antioch

The Jerusalem Council

Christianity reaches Rome?

Peter and Jude write to churches in Turkey

Peter and Paul die on Nero's orders

James and the Jerusalem believers flee to Pella before the Romans destroy the Jewish capital ugly story about animals and mythical beasts and unpleasant things happening, with everything turning out all right for God's people in the end.

Peter's first letter had contained reference to apocalyptic writings in a section that spoke of Jesus preaching to imprisoned spirits. Jude and 2 Peter contained much more of this stuff, and in order to get the point, the readers needed to know the code. We assume that the first readers did. Readers today need help – so reach for the commentaries and dig in!

A trip from the shadows to the light

Finally we come to the anonymous letter to the Hebrews. No-one knows who wrote this elegant, majestic letter on how the old covenant with the Jews was fulfilled in Jesus and the church. There has been no end of speculation as to whose pen it was: Paul (most unlikely), Luke, Silas, Barnabas (my favourite!), Apollos, Philip, Priscilla and Aquila. Certainly the author knew Timothy (see Hebrews 13:23), assumed to be the Timothy who was a colleague of Paul.   *(Hebrews 1:1–4)*

What is certain is that behind the pen was a great mind, thoroughly soaked in the Old Testament, capable of writing the finest Greek and able to show how Jesus fulfilled the highest aspirations of Judaism. It is almost certain that the letter was written to Jewish Christians – possibly ones who were wavering in their commitment to Jesus, feeling the pull of their old religion, much like John's first readers. However, the letter must have been written before the fall of Jerusalem and the destruction of the temple, since these events are not mentioned or even hinted at in it.   *(Hebrews 2:1–4)*

There are a variety of views on where the author lived and where the letter was sent to. The most probable is that it was sent to a group of Jewish Christians in Rome by a Jewish Christian living in one of the other main centres of church activity, possibly Ephesus, maybe Antioch.

It is a little misleading to describe Hebrews as a letter. It is rather a carefully constructed Bible study or sermon. It is based on four key Old Testament passages – Psalm 8, Psalm 95, Psalm 110 and Jeremiah 31:31–34 – and seeks to show how Jesus fulfils these texts.

So in chapters 1 and 2 Jesus is shown to be the fulfilment of Psalm 8. Chapters 3 and 4, based on Psalm 95, take up the theme of the redemption of God's people and the danger of hardening the heart, as Israel did in the wilderness. Chapters 5 to 7, based on Psalm 110, show how Jesus is both king and priest and has opened up a new way of approaching God. Chapters 8 to 10, based on Jeremiah 31, show how the new covenant in Jesus is greater than the old covenant it replaces. Chapters 11 to 13 contain the practical application and outworking of the meaty teaching contained in the first ten chapters. At all times the author is forcing his readers to dig deeper into the text of the Old Testament to find its true meaning revealed in Jesus, and hence to keep the faith that they seem to be in some danger of drifting away from.
(Hebrews 7:11–28)

Hebrews is undoubtedly one of the finest pieces of writing in the New Testament, but it is also one of the hardest to appreciate without a good working knowledge of the Old Testament. Getting the best out of Hebrews requires careful work with a concordance and a good commentary.

Getting the big picture

What James, Peter, Jude and the writer of Hebrews do is fill out the picture of salvation contained in the Gospels and the letters of Paul and John. God intends us to grasp the big picture, to see as clearly as possible the extent of the wonderful thing he has accomplished in Jesus. As the writer to the Hebrews says: 'We must pay greater attention to what we have heard, so that we do not drift away from it' (Hebrews 2:1). These varied writings help us to do just that.

For further thought

Read the letter of James and identify its major themes. Jot down what James says about the following:
(a) Suffering and testing.
(b) Wealth and possessions.
(c) Faith and works.
(d) Prayer and the Christian lifestyle.
   Take one item from each heading on your list and ask yourself:
(a) What does this say to me and my situation?
(b) How can I move from being a hearer of the Word to being a doer?

CHAPTER 9

■■■■■■■■■

Gentle thunder

John's letters

■■■■■■

*E*veryone, it seems, loves a mystery. TV detective shows, where the hero or heroine has to solve the mystery of 'whodunit', regularly top the ratings; crime and mystery novels sell in their tens of thousands; and *The Mousetrap*, an Agatha Christie mystery, is London theatreland's longest-running show, having been performed every night since the early 1950s.

The New Testament has its fair share of mysteries too. There are mysterious sayings in the Gospels – such as Jesus warning us not to give jewellery to pigs, or they might trample on it. There are strange events in Acts – like the death of Ananias and Sapphira or the effect of Peter's shadow on the sick. But one of the biggest mysteries in the New Testament is who wrote all the books that bear the name 'John'.

Did the same person write the Gospel, the three letters and Revelation? Did different people, each called John, write them? Is 'John' a name used by several people from the same church or group, in much the same way as

'Peterborough' in the *Daily Telegraph* or 'Pendennis' in the *Observer* are written by a number of people each week?

And possibly most interesting and mysterious of all, how is the 'John' who wrote these works connected to the John who was a follower of Jesus, the brother of James, the son of Zebedee, whom Jesus nicknamed 'thunderer'?

Back to school

In Chapter 3 we suggested that John's Gospel was written in the latter part of the first century by John Zebedee, who by that time was elderly and living in Ephesus. Nearly everyone agrees that the letters of John were written by the same hand that wrote the Gospel.

But there are other views. One very popular idea is that 'John' was a name used by a group of writers who

John's travels

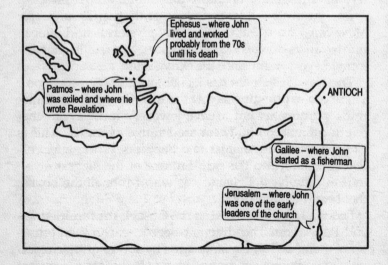

Ephesus – where John lived and worked probably from the 70s until his death

Patmos – where John was exiled and where he wrote Revelation

ANTIOCH

Galilee – where John started as a fisherman

Jerusalem – where John was one of the early leaders of the church had learned everything they knew of the Christian faith from John Zebedee. Some people have even suggested that there was a school – the first-century equivalent of a theological college – run by this old fisherman or in his name or memory.

This view accounts for the differences between the writings – especially between the Gospel and the letters on the one hand and Revelation on the other. Indeed, the original Greek of Revelation is so different from that of John's other works that many people suggest that they can't have come from the same person. But this isn't necessarily so, as we'll see in a moment.

There is something going for this idea of group authorship. In 1 John we frequently read phrases like 'we know' and 'we declare' rather than 'I know' and 'I declare'. This could be because the letter reflects the thinking of a group rather than an individual.   *(1 John 1 – 5)*

But there are major drawbacks to the idea of a school of John. One is that there is no evidence for its existence. No author writing in the second century, who refers to John, mentions a school or community. These people speak of John the apostle living in Ephesus and refer to him only in the context of being involved in the church – where, of course, he would have had a close circle of friends and fellow leaders.   *(1 John 1:1)*

A second drawback is that the writer of 1 John says that he is writing of what 'we have seen with our eyes, what we have looked at and touched with our hands'. This is the language of one or more eyewitnesses, not an expression meaning 'all of us at this school'.

And thirdly, the idea of a school of John doesn't make sense of the fact that the writer of 2 and 3 John refers to himself as 'the elder' and the writer of 1 John refers to his readers as 'dear children', 'beloved' and 'my little children'. This is not the language of a group of theological students! Rather, this is the kind of talk that we'd expect

111

from a venerable older leader, a grandfather, writing fondly to people he loves and cares for and has been working with over many years. It is possible to translate 'elder' as 'old man', as if the author is identifying himself by a title that everyone who knows him uses affectionately: 'the old man'.   *(1 John 2:1)*

The final drawback to the idea of John's writings being produced by a school is that Revelation just doesn't fit. This book (which we'll look at in more detail in the next chapter) is clearly the work of an isolated individual, someone cut off from the rest of the church who cannot be with the readers in person, though he wants to be.

Furthermore, Revelation is written by someone with authority, who can credibly claim that his words are inspired by God – that they are true prophecy, the reading of which will bring blessing. He also identifies himself simply as John. Only one of the original apostles could do this without having to justify himself – as Paul was constantly having to do.

But if Revelation is from the same hand as the letters and the Gospel, how come the style is so very different? This is very difficult to answer with any certainty. But it is not beyond the bounds of possibility that John had the help of a highly educated secretary in Ephesus who turned his somewhat ragged prose into the flat but competent, simple and uncluttered Greek of the Gospel and letters, whereas alone on Patmos he had to write as best he could.

On top of that, Revelation, being the report of a vision and being written in a particular kind of language which was comprehensible to those in the know but incomprehensible to their enemies, is a very different work from the Gospel and the letters, which were intended to teach plainly, if profoundly, about Jesus and the Christian life.

Such a view is not without problems, but it is entirely

plausible to suggest that the same hand wrote the Gospel, the letters and Revelation, and that that hand belonged to John Zebedee, who ended his days as the leader or a leading figure among a group of churches centred on Ephesus in the final decades of the first century. That is certainly the view we take in this chapter.

The heart of a pastor

The author of 2 and 3 John had a pastor's heart. He was deeply concerned for the health of the churches in his care. Ahead of a planned visit to two of them, he writes to encourage, reassure and warn. The fact that he was planning a visit at all at his age indicates the depth of his concern for these believing communities.

In 2 John he writes to a church which he describes as 'The elect lady and her children'. He encourages them to know and live by the truth of the gospel. He reassures them that they are going on well with the Lord. And he warns them against falling for false teaching.   (2 John 1, 4)

In 3 John he writes to Gaius, probably a leader of one of John's churches, about a letter he had sent to the church, which has been blocked by a member called Diotrephes. John's passion for the truth means that he must oppose this man, publicly if necessary, so that he does not have an undue influence over younger, more vulnerable believers.   (3 John 9–10)

In an age where everything is relative and people rely more on experience than on facts, John's emphasis on the truth, on holding firmly on to the facts of the faith, handed down from Jesus through the apostles, needs to be heard. But it needs to be heard correctly: John is not arguing for cold, unfeeling doctrine; rather, he is appealing for Christians to unite in love around the truth of the gospel; he is saying that the Holy Spirit inspires both great experiences and deep knowledge, ecstasy and education, love and truth, and that both are focused in John's master and friend, Jesus of Nazareth.

'Sorry, can you say that again?'

Love and truth come into sharp focus in 1 John. This is not so much a letter as a sermon that takes up various themes from John's Gospel, which some people had misunderstood. It is clear from the text that the readers of 1 John were being hassled by people teaching things which appeared to be very spiritual and based on the gospel but which were in fact drawn from pagan ideas.

We know what they were saying only by the way John answers them. It seems that the topics that 1 John addresses – fellowship with God, walking in the light, being children of God, being inspired by the Spirit – were all areas of interest to the false teachers. Apparently these people believed that the material world was hopelessly evil and didn't really matter to God. What counted was the 'spiritual' realm, the world of ideas and experiences. So to them 'truth' was any knowledge that unlocked the door to great experiences, ideas that freed the hearers from the physical nine-to-five, routine, workaday world that all of us live in.

To these people the great stress of John's Gospel that 'the Word became flesh and lived among us' couldn't be right. God would not get involved in the material order in that way. God was good, and thus could live only in the world of ideas, experience and knowledge.   (1 John 4:2)

So to get to know God required not the sacrifice of Christ on the cross to bear the punishment for our sins, but the gaining of special, secret knowledge about him that would unlock the door to a whole new world of spiritual experience and intimate union with him. Such knowledge could be acquired only from particular teachers, namely the people who had once been part of

John's church but had left and set up their own groups because what they taught contradicted the gospel John had learned from Jesus and the Holy Spirit. This way of understanding God and salvation grew in the second century into the full-blown alternative religion known as Gnosticism – a name derived from the Greek word for 'knowledge'.

John, of course, was not going to have any truck with nonsense like this. So 1 John takes up and develops themes from the Gospel which emphasize that Jesus came in the flesh, that it is his blood that cleanses our sins and that we can become children of God, people who live in the light, only through acknowledging our sin, allowing Jesus to wash us and make us whole and living our lives according to his teaching.   *(1 John 1:7)*

This very carefully structured letter falls into two halves. The first part, 1:5 – 2:29, could be headed 'God is light'. God is totally holy, pure and good, and therefore we, his people, should live in the light of that and seek to be holy, pure and good ourselves through following Jesus. Then, under a heading of 'God is our Father', 3:1 – 5:12 tells us that God loves us and is gracious and generous towards us, and that we should therefore live lives that honour him, our heavenly parent, out of gratitude for all that he's done for us.

In each half John makes the same five basic points. He tells his readers to renounce sin (1:8 – 2:2; 3:4–9); to be obedient to the truth (2:3–11; 3:10–24); to reject ideas and lifestyles that owe their origin to the world's way of thinking rather than to the gospel of Jesus Christ (2:12–17; 4:1–6); to love, accept and care for one another (1:5–7; 4:7 – 5:4); and to keep the faith they learned from him – especially when under pressure from the false teachers to reject it (2:18–29; 5:5–13).

This is all wrapped up in an introduction (1:1–4) and a conclusion (5:14–21) that assure us that if we live like this we will have fellowship with the Father and with one another, which means that we will be absolutely secure in a difficult world, enjoying the support of brothers and sisters in the church and the constant presence of God through answered prayer.

The wisdom of age

John knows just how hard life is. He's the kind of person who comes and sits with you after church, listens to your struggles and then prays with a simple wisdom that brings a sense of perspective and peace. John calls us back to basics with a gentle but firm voice that has been fine-tuned by experience. The bumptious, arrogant disciple who asked for the most important place at Christ's side has been tempered into the humble, wise pastor who knows that very few things in life are certain, but that Christians need to hold on to those few certainties, no matter what.

His writings – especially 1 John – distil the wisdom of age with a clarity and winsomeness that bring us to the heart of the matter: Jesus is the truth, love is the way, and life is about growing up in the light of those two certainties.

For further thought

A recently published book on John and his church was called *Thunder and Love*, because this title expresses the two key themes in John's writings: passion for the truth and compassion for people.

Read 1 John and list all the verses that show John's passion for truth and his compassionate feelings towards people. Could these two words – thunder and love – be used to sum up your faith?

CHAPTER 10
■■■■■■■■■

Seeing with your ears

Reading Revelation without going crazy

As we left the cinema, the strains of the rock group The Doors and gunfire dying in our ears, I turned to my friend and said, 'Well, what on earth was that all about?' We had been sitting through *Apocalypse Now*, Francis Ford Coppola's epic interpretation of the Vietnam War, and my head was spinning.

As we sat in the pub afterwards, my friend and I tried to fathom out what the film was about. I knew that it was loosely based on Joseph Conrad's *Heart of Darkness*, as well as being about the war in South East Asia that had visited my living room every evening when I was a teenager.

Coppola's picture made an immediate impact – noise, confusion, fear, anger, laughter and madness. But I found its impact growing, maturing into something deeper and more satisfying as I thought about particular scenes and incidents in the film and tried to grasp how they related to the whole. It also helped to see it again.

John's apocalypse – more commonly called Revelation

– is a little like Coppola's *Apocalypse Now*. It is full of weird goings-on: angels with bowls and trumpets, mothers snatched up into heaven, beasts rising from the sea, people identified by numbers, and saints crammed under altars wailing for revenge. It seems to rush from one thing to the next without pausing to allow the reader to catch her breath. And a common reaction on reaching the end is to gasp for air and say, 'Well, what on earth was that all about?'

Of course, bewilderment has not stopped people from pontificating on what Revelation is about. From Hal Lindsey's *The Late Great Planet Earth* to D. H. Lawrence's *Apocalypse*, all sorts of people have put pen to paper to tell us what the book means.

But what are you?

In one scene in Disney's *Alice in Wonderland* a marvellous mauve caterpillar keeps asking Alice, 'Who are you?' The trouble is that after spending so long in Wonderland, Alice isn't too sure. Many people who read Revelation aren't too sure exactly what it is they are reading. Some read it thinking it is a wonderful, if puzzling, picture of heaven, the victory of Jesus and the future of his people; others think it's a lucky dip of predictions which can be used like a railway timetable. Some don't bother to read it at all.

Everyone knows that Romans is a letter, Mark is a gospel and the Psalms are poems. But what is Revelation? It starts like a letter (1:4), claims to be a prophecy (1:3) and is in fact an example of the genre of Jewish and Christian writings known as apocalyptic, a type of literature characterized by garish images and concern for God's honour and for the future of his people. (The Greek word in 1:1 translated 'revelation' is also the origin of our word 'apocalyptic'.)

The easy answer to this question, favoured by an

The seven churches of Revelation

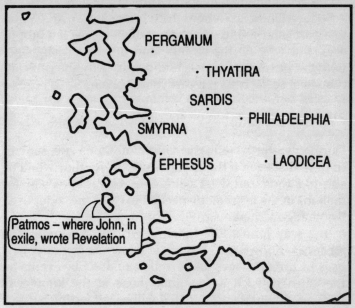

PERGAMUM

· THYATIRA

SARDIS

· PHILADELPHIA

SMYRNA

·EPHESUS

· LAODICEA

Patmos – where John, in exile, wrote Revelation

increasing number of people, is to say that Revelation is all three – a letter, a prophecy and an apocalypse. But this doesn't help us very much.

Perhaps we should come at it from the other end and ask: 'Who was it written for?' John tells us that he was writing for the seven churches in the Roman province of Asia (*i.e.* the south-western part of what we call Turkey), one of which was in Ephesus. In the previous chapter we saw that John's ministry was centred on Ephesus. John tells us further that he is writing from Patmos, an island off the coast of Turkey, where, it seems, he had been exiled or imprisoned because of his preaching.   (*Revelation 1:4*)

On top of that, John describes what he writes as the Word of God to these churches. He tells his readers that they will be blessed if they hear and obey the words they read. And he tells them that what he has written will give them insight into what is going on now, both on earth in their own neighbourhoods and in heaven.

So Revelation is a letter which brings the Word of God to a particular group of people (which makes it a prophecy). But why all the strange and unsettling language, why the pictures of angels and beasts, why the constant change of scene between earth and heaven?

Cracking the code

During wartime, military communications are sent in code so that even if the enemy eavesdrops, they won't be able to fathom out what's going on. Governments invest millions in the technology needed to crack the codes used by other governments.

In a way John's Revelation is written in a code. The form of writing used – which is known as apocalyptic – uses pictures, images and symbols to describe events on the earth in such a way that those in the know will understand but the uninitiated will be left feeling baffled. There are many works written in this way dating from around 200 BC to AD 200. John's Revelation was probably written between AD 80 and 95.

One clear example of the code at work in Revelation is the description of a city which John calls Babylon. In Jewish thinking Babylon, which had long since ceased to be a city of any power or importance, had become a symbol for the political oppression and persecution of God's people. This is because it was Babylon that had defeated Israel, overthrown Jerusalem and carted the Jews off into exile in 587 BC.   *(Revelation 18)*

Now Rome was the dominant power on the world's stage, and it persecuted the people of God. It had taken Babylon's place, and in apocalyptic writing it was given Babylon's name too. So when John wrote about Babylon in chapters 17 and 18, his readers would have understood that he was speaking about Rome. But when his Roman jailers looked at what he was writing, they would have just assumed that he was engaging in a bit of fantasy from Israel's past.

Our trouble with Revelation is often that we don't know the code. Many of its symbols are obscure and difficult, so to get the most from John's work, we need to have a commentary close at hand.

A postcard from the margin

John lived in dangerous times. His congregations faced threats from within through the activities of false teachers, and from without through opposition from Jews and the Roman authorities. And he could not be with them to encourage them and to help them keep their eyes on things above and not be crushed by the pressures around them. So he dropped them a postcard from Patmos. He didn't write a letter like Philippians or even 1 John. Rather, he sent something visual. It seems that he wanted his people to 'see' with their ears and so grasp what was happening around them.

When we read Revelation it is important for us to remember that this letter was written in response to the circumstances of its original readers and in such a way that it addressed their needs – just as 1 Corinthians responded to particular problems in the church at Corinth. But instead of writing a straightforward letter, John wrote an apocalypse. As we have seen, this was partly to protect the content of his message. After all, one of his key themes is that Jesus is king and that any others who claim that title – the Roman Emperor included – are imposters. Worse, as far as the Romans were concerned, John likened their regime to a beast, a prostitute and the great oppressor Babylon. And finally, he assured his readers that God was coming to sweep this corrupt empire away. In short, John was writing treason, so it's little wonder that he used code.

But the other reason for writing an apocalypse was that

John knew that sometimes mere exhortation, however inspired, just isn't enough. People need a picture, a fresh way of seeing the world as it really is, that will inspire them to endure hardship. In this way Revelation is a bit like the section of Isaiah that begins in chapter 40 and ends in chapter 55 and is clearly written to be relevant to the people of God in exile in Babylon. That passage is not a sermon, or a carefully reasoned theology of God's sovereignty, but a poem. There were the people, languishing in exile, abandoning their faith, despairing of ever seeing home again – and God sends a poet.

The reason was simple: what the people needed was to have their eyes lifted to see the world in a different way, to disregard the distorted message that came through the world around them and from their neighbours and even from their own sinful imaginations, and to see the world as God saw it. Isaiah 40 – 55 did that for the people of Israel in exile. And Revelation did it for the seven churches in Turkey at the tail-end of the first century.

Making it make sense

One of my favourite films is *Excalibur*, John Boorman's interpretation of the legend of King Arthur. When I have an evening in alone, I often put it on and watch some or all of it. Every time I watch it I find something new in it. There is a great scene after the grail has been brought to Arthur by Percival, and the restored King rides out to meet Mordred for the final battle. They leave the castle and enter a barren, wintry landscape. But as the King and his knights gallop through a glade, spring breaks out, leaves and flowers appear, and by the end of the scene you can hardly see the horsemen for the blossom. The symbolism is obvious – that the King and the land are one, that the land can flourish only if the King does. But it took me a number of viewings to see it and to recognize the part it plays in telling the story of the film.

Revelation is similar. It needs to be read and reread in order to make sense. As you reread it you notice recurring themes, groups of words, numbers, objects – you begin to see how the end relates to the beginning, how what happens in heaven relates to things happening on earth. Revelation is not a book that yields its treasure on first acquaintance. So for Revelation to make sense to us, it is essential for us to read it many times.

It is also important that we learn to handle the symbolism properly. Because John is trying to make his readers see with their ears, nearly everything he says, he says by using a picture or a symbol.

Firstly, we need to look for parallels between John's symbols and the pictures we find in the Old Testament. No other New Testament writer quotes or refers to the Old Testament as much as John. Indeed, he seems consciously to have modelled what he says on the Old Testament, so that everything he writes is a fulfilment of and a climax to what appears in the Hebrew Bible.

So, the living creatures of chapter 4 are drawn from Ezekiel's vision, the white hair of Christ in chapter 1 reminds us of Daniel's picture of the Ancient of Days, and the 12,000 from each of the twelve tribes in chapters 7 and 14 speak of the totality of the people of God.   *(Ezekiel 1:10; Daniel 7:13–14)*

When we come across a symbol we should ask ourselves whether John draws it from the Old Testament. But we should not assume that it has exactly the same meaning for John that it had for the Old Testament writer, because John reinterprets everything in his Bible in the light of Christ's coming and coronation.

Secondly, we need to be careful with the details of the symbols. John is an artist who paints in broad brushstrokes. For example, he does not expect us to find a meaning for each of the eyes belonging to the living creatures in chapter 4.

Thirdly, we need to understand the symbols not solely

in their own right but also in terms of their context within the whole work. So the beast is not one person and Babylon something else; both are symbols of Rome. John is using a variety of pictures to help his readers to see clearly what they are up against, and he shows them the Roman Empire in all its economic, spiritual and military ugliness. *(Revelation 17, 18)*

Fourthly, we need to guard against thinking that the symbols or pictures can be reduced to simple 'this = that' statements. What John does in chapter 1 is to make a stab at describing what he saw. That's why he keeps saying that things were like other things. If we reduce his pictures to a set of propositions, we end up with John saying that Jesus is an ancient white-haired man with fluorescent tubes for eyes and a shaft of steel protruding from between his lips.

The final key to making sense of Revelation is to recognize what the book is about. It is not about the future, the millennium or the judgment. Still less has it anything to do with the forming of the European Union, the Cold War, Saddam Hussein or the bar-coding of groceries! Revelation is about Jesus Christ. This is clear from the first sentence. But to reinforce it, John's first vision is of the risen and exalted Christ who is the beginning and the end of the matter, the one who holds the keys to life and death and the one who rules on earth. And his vision of heaven has at its heart the worship of the slain Lamb, the one who has ransomed people from sin by the shedding of his blood. *(Revelation 1; 5:1–14)*

Bringing order out of chaos

On the first reading Revelation just seems to be a mass of happenings and random events. That, of course, is very much like life. The world of Revelation's first readers must have seemed harsh and bewildering. They lived in a world that was decidedly unfriendly towards their new faith. They experienced opposition and persecution that at times must have made them wonder whether there was a God at all, let alone one who was on their side and in control.

But as we read and reread this powerful work, an order appears – not just on the page but also in our lives. In the midst of the haphazard events, the twists of fate, the good and bad luck, the evil of people and the suffering of the innocent, stands Jesus. He is both the slain Lamb – the picture of innocent suffering and sacrificial death – and the rider on the white horse who conquers and wears the crown.   (*Revelation 6:2*)

And standing with Jesus are his people. They are not passively observing what's happening – they are in the thick of the battle, and their task is to tell the world who Jesus is so that it might avoid the miseries and terrors of judgment. Indeed, one of the purposes which John seems to have in mind in writing Revelation is to tell his people to keep the faith and to keep proclaiming the good news of Jesus, even at the cost of losing their lives, because that will bring glory and great honour to the Lamb who was slain.

Who's calling the shots here?

When Ronald Reagan was shot and wounded early in his first term as President of the USA, confusion reigned. Vice-President George Bush told the world, 'I'm in charge.' At the same time Secretary of State Al Haig held a press conference to announce that he was in charge. The upshot was that no-one knew whose finger was on the trigger of the world's largest nuclear stockpile. For a few hours everyone held their breath: the world was out of control.

The message of Revelation is 'I'm in charge.' At the end of the first century, as Roman Emperors demanded more and more to be worshipped as gods and as their officials grew more hostile to the Christian church because believers refused to say 'Caesar is Lord', Jesus came to his friend John to remind him who really calls the shots in the universe.

Revelation contains God's final word about human life, history and destiny. That's why it ended up as the last book of the Bible. For just as Genesis opens the Bible with an account of creation, so Revelation closes it with an account of the new creation. Just as the New Testament opens with four accounts of the earthly life and ministry of Jesus, so it closes with an account of Jesus as the King of the universe and the Lord of history.

All that the Old Testament set the scene for is fulfilled in Jesus, says John. All that happens to the church – good and bad – is in the hands of Jesus who, through the church, proclaims the message, 'I'm in charge. Look to me and live,' and to whom the church in worship and adoration says, 'Amen. Come, Lord Jesus.'

For further thought

Using a concordance, find all the references in Revelation to:
(a) the lordship of Jesus.
(b) the testimony/witness/martyrdom of Christians.

What do we learn from these texts about the nature and role of the church in the world? (This is a difficult question, because the texts contain many strange pictures and images that are hard to understand. You will get the most out of this exercise if you concentrate closely on the question and don't allow yourself to get sidetracked by weird things!)

CHAPTER 11

■ ■ ■ ■ ■ ■ ■ ■ ■

A standard to live by

■■■■■■

As the second Christian century dawned, all the apostles – the witnesses of Jesus' life and ministry – were dead and gone. Other people who had been involved from the earliest days of the new movement were also dying off. The need was growing for a body of teaching that everyone could trust, a reliable record of what Jesus had said and done and what the apostles had taught about him.

The simplest way of keeping that record was in written form. After all, the church had inherited what we call the Old Testament from the Jews. It made sense, therefore, to put alongside these writings the texts that preserved and communicated the truth about Jesus.

But which writings? By the end of the first century there were probably hundreds of letters, books, sermons, apocalypses and documents of various kinds about Jesus or his followers. Which ones told the truth, the whole truth and nothing but the truth?

Some of the twenty-seven books that make up our New Testament were regarded as special almost from the day they were written. Many of Paul's letters, for instance, were being treated as Scripture even during Paul's lifetime, as Peter observes in his second letter, written before AD 64. He tells his readers that some of what Paul says is difficult to grasp, and that people are inclined to twist what he's saying to suit their purposes, 'as they do the *other* Scriptures'. In other words, 'Take Paul seriously; his words are inspired by God.'   (2 *Peter 3:16*)

It is likely that John's Gospel was very quickly seen to have the mark of truth about it. The other three Gospels seem to have rapidly established themselves as having a unique authority, despite the fact that many 'lives of Jesus' had been written, as Luke mentions at the beginning of his account.

So, how shall we decide, then?

But what was it that made these books special? Three things seem to have worked together to persuade the leaders of the church in the second and third centuries that the books of our New Testament were uniquely authoritative.

The first mark that people looked for was some connection with an apostle. It was to the twelve apostles that Jesus had entrusted the job of preaching the good news about himself and teaching people all that he had taught. To the Twelve Jesus added Paul, the one he called after his resurrection with the special job of opening up the church to the Gentiles. Writings that were connected with these people were likely to have the ring of truth about them. So it is not surprising that probably by the end of the first century, and certainly by the middle of the second, the thirteen letters that bear Paul's name were being treated as Scripture alongside the Old Testament. So too were the four Gospels, John's because it was written by the apostle, Matthew's likewise (though that has always been questioned), Mark's because he was associated with Peter, and Luke's because he was a colleague of Paul. Alongside those, 1 Peter and 1 John were very quickly regarded as special, because they were written by apostles, as was the Acts of the Apostles, because it was written by Luke.

The other seven New Testament books – Hebrews, James, 2 Peter, 2 and 3 John, Jude and Revelation – were accepted in some churches but not others. There were problems with them that had to be resolved before they could be accepted by everyone. Hebrews, for instance, was anonymous, so it was very hard to link it with an apostle. There were doubts about 2 Peter and Jude, since they quoted from books that were not in the Old Testament and seemed to be treating them as Scripture. James had not been an apostle and, as the church grew in the Gentile world and shrank in the Jewish world, his association with Jerusalem and Judaism was viewed with a little suspicion.

The second test which was applied to books to see whether they met the mark and could be treated as Scripture was whether they taught the truth or not. Many of the writings circulating in the second and third centuries contained things about Jesus that were right, but they also contained material that ranged from interesting speculation to complete nonsense, and so they were deemed to be unhelpful in teaching the truth. After all, Scripture was meant to be truth that helped people to grow in their understanding of God and salvation. Writing that didn't do that couldn't be Scripture. But the seven books about which there were doubts certainly did help people to grow as Christians.

Now, that's inspired!

The third test was linked to the second, and it had to do with the effects which a particular book or letter had on its readers. Do I feel God speaking to me as I read it? Am I able to base decisions on its teaching? Would I trust my life to these words? Does following this teaching lead to God blessing me and my church? These questions are subjective but important. This third test, linked with the other two, worked to bring together the books that make up our New Testament, because the overwhelming majority of Christians felt that these writings were especially inspired by God, just as the Old Testament was.

It was not until the fourth century that a formal list of the twenty-seven books was drawn up. It is called the canon of the New Testament, 'canon' meaning 'rule' or 'standard'. But all that happened in the fourth century was that the church formally recognized what the Holy Spirit had been telling them for a very long time: these books are special; read them, trust them, live by them.

CHAPTER 12

■■■■■■■■■

Rolling up your shirt-sleeves

_____

*N*ow that we've got ourselves a bit of background to these books and a few pointers to how we should approach them, we need to get down to the most important thing we can do with the New Testament: reading it!

Here's a reading plan for you to follow. There's a chunk of the New Testament to read every day and a box to tick when you've read it. If you miss a day, don't abandon the whole project – just pick it up again where you left off.

It's probably a good idea to have a notebook handy to jot down questions or quotes that you found particularly helpful. You should also have a Bible dictionary or commentary handy to look up anything you don't understand – don't stay in the dark or guess.

The plan takes you through the New Testament in just under five months. Some readings are long chunks, others are short passages – for variety. The plan doesn't follow the order of our Bibles but mixes up history, letters and authors – again for variety.

Sometimes it's good to read with a friend so that you can encourage one another when enthusiasm wanes.

Finally, a word of warning: reading the New Testament can and will seriously change your life and affect the lives of everyone you come into contact with. Through it God will work to remould you in the image of its central character, Jesus Christ.

So read it, expecting God to speak to you; listen carefully to what he says, enjoy it, seek to understand it and, above all, live it.

Jesus, the Messiah, fulfils the Old Testament

Day 1	Matthew 1 – 4	☐
Day 2	Matthew 5 – 7	☐
Day 3	Matthew 8 – 10	☐
Day 4	Matthew 11 – 14	☐
Day 5	Matthew 15 – 20	☐
Day 6	Matthew 21 – 25	☐
Day 7	Matthew 26 – 28	☐

God creates a new people out of both Jews and Gentiles

Day 8	Romans 1 – 4	☐
Day 9	Romans 5 – 8	☐
Day 10	Romans 9 – 11	☐
Day 11	Romans 12 – 16	☐
Day 12	James 1 – 2	☐
Day 13	James 3 – 5	☐
Day 14	Jude	☐

Jesus: man of power

Day 15	Mark 1 – 3	☐
Day 16	Mark 4	☐
Day 17	Mark 5 – 6	☐

Day 18	Mark 7 – 8	☐
Day 19	Mark 9 – 10	☐
Day 20	Mark 11 – 13	☐
Day 21	Mark 14 – 16	☐

The church in the raw

Day 22	1 Corinthians 1 – 4	☐
Day 23	1 Corinthians 5 – 7	☐
Day 24	1 Corinthians 8 – 11	☐
Day 25	1 Corinthians 12 – 14	☐
Day 26	1 Corinthians 15 – 16	☐
Day 27	Philippians 1 – 2	☐
Day 28	Philippians 3 – 4	☐

God completes everything in Jesus, his Son

Day 29	Hebrews 1 – 2	☐
Day 30	Hebrews 3 – 4	☐
Day 31	Hebrews 5 – 7	☐
Day 32	Hebrews 8 – 10	☐
Day 33	Hebrews 11	☐
Day 34	Hebrews 12	☐
Day 35	Hebrews 13	☐

Jesus: the Saviour of the world

Day 36	Luke 1 – 3	☐
Day 37	Luke 4 – 5	☐
Day 38	Luke 6	☐
Day 39	Luke 7 – 8	☐
Day 40	Luke 9 – 10	☐
Day 41	Luke 11 – 13	☐
Day 42	Luke 14	☐
Day 43	Luke 15	☐
Day 44	Luke 16 – 17	☐

Day 45	Luke 18	☐
Day 46	Luke 19	☐
Day 47	Luke 20 – 21	☐
Day 48	Luke 22 – 23	☐
Day 49	Luke 24	☐

God is faithful in all life's trials

Day 50	2 Corinthians 1 – 2	☐
Day 51	2 Corinthians 3 – 4	☐
Day 52	2 Corinthians 5	☐
Day 53	2 Corinthians 6 – 7	☐
Day 54	2 Corinthians 8 – 9	☐
Day 55	2 Corinthians 10 – 11	☐
Day 56	2 Corinthians 12 – 13	☐

Live a good life and wait for your King

Day 57	1 Peter 1	☐
Day 58	1 Peter 2	☐
Day 59	1 Peter 3	☐
Day 60	1 Peter 4	☐
Day 61	1 Peter 5	☐
Day 62	2 Peter 1	☐
Day 63	2 Peter 2 – 3	☐

God becomes a man to rescue us

Day 64	John 1 – 2	☐
Day 65	John 3	☐
Day 66	John 4	☐
Day 67	John 5 – 6	☐
Day 68	John 7 – 9	☐
Day 69	John 10	☐
Day 70	John 11	☐
Day 71	John 12	☐

Day 72	John 13 – 14	☐
Day 73	John 15 – 16	☐
Day 74	John 17	☐
Day 75	John 18 – 19	☐
Day 76	John 20	☐
Day 77	John 21	☐

Going to the ends of the earth

Day 78	Acts 1 – 5	☐
Day 79	Acts 6 – 8:3	☐
Day 80	Acts 8:4 – 9	☐
Day 81	Acts 10 – 11	☐
Day 82	Acts 12 – 14	☐
Day 83	Acts 15	☐
Day 84	Acts 16	☐

Day 85	Acts 17	☐
Day 86	Acts 18 – 19	☐
Day 87	Acts 20	☐
Day 88	Acts 21 – 22	☐
Day 89	Acts 23	☐
Day 90	Acts 24	☐
Day 91	Acts 25 – 26	☐

Jesus sets us free to serve him

Day 92	Galatians 1 – 2	☐
Day 93	Galatians 3	☐
Day 94	Galatians 4 – 5	☐
Day 95	Galatians 6	☐
Day 96	Titus 1	☐
Day 97	Titus 2	☐
Day 98	Titus 3	☐

Keep a firm hold on the truth

Day 99	1 John 1 – 2	☐
Day 100	1 John 3	☐
Day 101	1 John 4	☐
Day 102	1 John 5	☐
Day 103	2 and 3 John	☐
Day 104	1 Timothy 1 – 3	☐
Day 105	1 Timothy 4 – 6	☐

Keep holding on – Jesus is coming

Day 106	1 Thessalonians 1 – 2	☐
Day 107	1 Thessalonians 3 – 4	☐
Day 108	2 Thessalonians 1 – 3	☐
Day 109	2 Timothy 1	☐
Day 110	2 Timothy 2	☐
Day 111	2 Timothy 3	☐
Day 112	2 Timothy 4	☐

Jesus is Lord of heaven, earth and the church

Day 113	Revelation 1 – 3	☐
Day 114	Revelation 4 – 5	☐
Day 115	Revelation 6 – 7	☐
Day 116	Revelation 8 – 9	☐
Day 117	Revelation 10	☐
Day 118	Revelation 11 – 12	☐
Day 119	Revelation 13	☐
Day 120	Revelation 14 – 15	☐
Day 121	Revelation 16 – 17	☐
Day 122	Revelation 18 – 20	☐
Day 123	Revelation 21 – 22	☐
Day 124	Ephesians 1	☐
Day 125	Ephesians 2	☐
Day 126	Ephesians 3	☐

Jesus, name above all names

Ten useful books

The NIV Study Bible (Hodder & Stoughton, 1987).

The Message by Eugene Peterson (Navpress, 1993) – a wonderful, fresh, vigorous paraphrase of the New Testament.

The New Bible Dictionary/Illustrated Bible Dictionary (IVP, 1982).

The New Bible Commentary (21st-century edition, IVP, 1994).

Bethlehem to Patmos: The New Testament Story by Paul Barnett (Hodder & Stoughton, 1989).

New Testament History by F. F. Bruce (Marshall Pickering, 3rd Edition, 1982).

The Historical Reliability of the Gospels by Craig Blomberg (IVP, 1987).

Taking the Guesswork out of Applying the Bible by Jack Kuhatschek (IVP, 1990).

Seeing in the Dark by Philip Yancey (Marshall Pickering, 1988) – a terrific overview of the Bible's story, including the New Testament (in parts 3 and 4): a wonderful, faith-building read.

Praying with Jesus by Eugene Peterson (HarperCollins, 1993) – a year of meditations and prayers taking the reader through Matthew and John.